Lig_ L L & wise

How to be your own Soul Whisperer
and liberate yourself from fear and illusion

Light-filled, Loving & Wise
How to be your own Soul Whisperer and liberate yourself
from fear and illusion

©Anna-Louise Haigh

ISBN: 978-1906316-64-8

Published in 2010 by HotHive Books, Evesham, UK.
www.thehothive.com

The right of Anna-Louise Haigh to be identified as
the author of this work has been asserted by her in
accordance with the Copyright, Designs and Patents Act
1988.

A CIP record of this book is available from the British
Library.

Printed in the UK by Latimer Trend, Plymouth

This book is dedicated to you and the enrichment of your journey through your increased magnificence.

Let the world be brighter through the radiance of your smile.

Contents

Acknowledgements . . . .

When a book I am writing is taking shape it becomes a living part of my life. This means that I once again need to thank my family, friends, clients, students, and my partner for creating the space in which this treasury of wisdom could be birthed.

I am tremendously grateful for the time and contributions of my test readers: Sharon Coleman, Debbie Wolstenholme, Anna Guttoriello, Silvana Minto, Caroline Hulme, Helen Connor, Marie Kerry, Andree Taylor, Mel Taylor, and Lena Bryant.

Special thanks must go to Karen Swinden, Sara Drinkwater, Cara Carey and the rest of the HotHive publishing team for their enthusiasm, guidance and professionalism in bringing this book into the reality you hold.

Preface

> *'If we knew all the answers, we would live beyond the stars'*
> Anna-Louise Haigh

Why? Why? Why? Do you remember asking this all the time when you were a child? Every time you ask this most powerful question you are on the verge of growing within your knowledge, consciousness and understanding of yourself and of life.

It is a natural human desire to want to gain understanding and know the answers to the questions that most often begin with why. Sometimes, perhaps your question was just one word, 'Why?'

Does the need to know come from within you or from the experiences that seem to repeat themselves over and over again in your life? Are you looking for explanations, understanding, answers or opportunities to start to make changes, or all of the above? And if this question originates within you, where are the answers coming from? Your head? Your heart? Your soul? Your inner child? Your day-time or night-time dreams? Or your feelings that life should just be better than this?

For some, the motivation to find the answers may be the quest for release from years of guilt, anger, grief, fear or regret. For others it may be to bring meaning to life events so that healing can begin. There are inevitably those who need a starting point for a new beginning or at least a closing of a chapter. And yet for others it may be to find clarity and direction through determining their life purpose.

My name is Anna-Louise. Some say I should be called Anna-Lytical because I am a spiritual sleuth when it comes to discovering the reason behind events, actions and behaviour. In this book, I will share with you the secrets, wisdoms, and tools that I know can successfully help you make sense of your experiences. What's more, in gaining these invaluable insights, you will be able to liberate yourself from the energy link that may be holding you in unsatisfactory repeated patterns, unfulfilling work, and relationships that no longer 'sparkle'. Ultimately you will meet the wonderful soul that you host, which makes you the amazing person you truly are.

Whatever the motivation, you are not alone in having questions arising out of your experiences, the answers to which will help you move forward and create a better life. So what is your reason?

At some level you know you need to find the meaning and yet there may be a subtle subconscious 'safety-net' that has stopped you in the past. Perhaps this was through fear of what might be revealed or the fear of change. 'No sense in opening up old wounds', you might hear echoing between your ears. Who said that? And why? I strongly advocate that self-empowerment and life fulfilment are gained by living in the here and now. In addition, the potential to positively engage with this 'power' is easily accessible within you. Yet to get to that place, you do have to lay to rest the 'gremlins' that freeload on your memories and cause you to linger in un-serving beliefs, behaviour patterns, and expectations. If you feel you have given away your power during your life, and you are ready to reclaim it through deeper understanding of the meaning behind your experiences, then you are reading the right book at the right time.

What you call 'your life' is in fact a journey of self-discovery. Every day presents opportunities to grow just that little bit more. If you feel you have missed out on this so far, it may be because you have, for some reason, silenced the messages around you and from within you. However, my guess is that you picked up this book because you were 'nudged'. And that means that the voice from within is ready once again to be heard and, as you know, timing is everything.

Before we start, let me just say this, this book is intended to be a pocket-size treasury that you can benefit from, by keeping it with you, for when you need it most. I became my own Soul Whisperer in order to be able to make sense of my experiences. Everything I deliver in this book has come from personal experience in one way or another. My own personal and soul growth journey, enhanced through working with my clients and students, has put my professional training in various spiritual psychology, healing, and metaphysical approaches to excellent use. This journey has helped me validate who I am and why I am here. The results I deliver speak for themselves.

For many years, the number of well-respected exponents of personal growth, inner healing, life alignment, and manifesting the best life possible, has been growing. Perhaps you have explored some of them and have absorbed some nuggets that have helped you along the way. Like you, I am on a journey. This adventure into understanding, knowing, healing, releasing, enabling, self-empowerment and self-honouring has brought unimaginable rewards. It can do the same for you.

I will endeavour wholeheartedly to awaken within you a treasury of life enrichment, based on the best (or worst, depending on your viewpoint) that my life and career experiences have brought me. Without doubt, this book was written for you.

To open this next avenue along your own personal journey, you need to bear in mind the following two important things.

Firstly, I can only speak from my viewpoint, born from my experiences. These may echo your encounters, yet they can never be completely the same, so I encourage you to season what is in this book with your own unique life experience 'flavourings', so that you gain the best for yourself and your understanding.

Secondly, not everything I say will resonate with you. That is absolutely fine and enhances my first point. Embrace that which rings true for you and let the rest go. However, I would ask you to remain open to the possibility that the information that resonates less readily now may, in time, contain a jewel of understanding.

Remember that every time you ask, 'Why?', you are on the crest of a new wave of adventure. When you have learned to become your own Soul Whisperer you will confidently know how to ride that wave and be grateful for the opportunity.

I came across a greeting card, when I was about 14 years old, that contained a verse with the title 'A child becomes what it lives'. It made a great deal of sense and basically said that a parent hosts a child's development rather than owning their life. It described situations, circumstances, and emotional environments in which the child becomes the product of its experiences. This is where a lot of your beliefs, ideas, approaches and responses to life events are created. 'Yes' I thought, 'someone, somewhere gets it; now, if only I could get this message in front of the right set of eyes at home, my life might blossom', but that was not to be at that time.

As you read this book, you will realise that you are not alone in your experiences. That someone really does understand, and what's more, is here to help you grow, heal and live the life you were meant to.

It was my early years that opened up my resourcefulness both psychologically and spiritually to become a Soul Whisperer. I consider this the best possible training for the life's work I passionately embrace, which is to inform, guide, heal, inspire and empower the unique person you are, through igniting your heart (and soul) into the light-filled, loving and wise person you were born to be. I honour your radiance and support your happiness, abundance and success, wherever your heart leads you.

Now it is your turn.

Anna-Louise Haigh
Harrogate, England 2010

Introduction

No matter who you are, we all start somewhere with the threads (thoughts) that will become the story we weave about our life.

On so many occasions you will have picked up these threads from the tail ends of those around you. Have you ever questioned whether what you are being offered is in alignment with your own truth or will lead you to lasting happiness?

The point is that the pursuit of happiness, love, life-satisfaction, respect, confidence, success or appreciation can only be manifested into reality if we first recognise where these particular attributes (and many more) exist within us. Otherwise, how will you recognise them when you find them, if you haven't already acknowledged and experienced them from within?

It is natural to carry the memories, thoughts and, consequently, the beliefs that were infused into you during your early years. You do this without questioning because you trust the source. You have probably temporarily shut down the ability to truly connect with your inner consciousness, which is there to guide you.

So often, what you were told about yourself as a young child comes from the deep inner, often subconscious, opinions your parents, family, teachers and other significant people in your life felt about themselves and how they thought the world treated them. Thankfully, in many cases, these echoes were of attributes that are confidence building, such as love (ideally unconditional), trust, loyalty, support, stability and nurturing. Yet, unfortunately, so often what you were told about yourself comes from the frustrations, perceived failures, inadequacies, misguided views of reality and unresolved issues harboured by those who imparted their words to you. You trusted these people to tell you the truth and therefore when they delivered their 'message' you believed them.

Perhaps, initially, you thought they were wrong, but then, with repeated reinforcement, you started to wonder if they were right. Gradually you came to believe what was said of you, your abilities and your potential, and as a result you may have questioned whether you were even lovable or deserved anything good in life.

I am asked regularly, what inspired me to become a Soul Whisperer and write a book by that name. It took me a long time before I could answer that question in a way that really expressed what made me sit down and take on the challenge. The answer was that my life has presented a myriad of situations and challenges, which collectively most people would consider unbelievable for one person to experience in one lifetime. I needed to find the answers to my questions. Over my years as a therapist and healer, meeting many people with similar unanswered questions who were searching for answers and release from their 'story', I realised that I was not alone and could offer a way forward. I had learned how to make sense of my life experiences and the time came when The Soul Whisperer had to be written. I had ignored the nudges for a long time and then they became more like a shove. In seeking understanding, I found a way of looking at my experiences, those of my clients and students, and global occurrences, that allowed me to make sense of it all.

I became aware of the physical sensations that happened when I received a piece of information, which seemed to come from nowhere and arrive within my consciousness, that untangled the meaning behind a situation or event and allowed the healing to begin.

Light-filled, Loving & Wise is a synergy of collective real-life experiences gained through my own, my clients' and my students' encounters, along with a different view to some of the meatier situations in life. I will offer you suggestions and various solutions that you can use whenever you need to continue to release yourself from fear and illusion.

No doubt you will find yourself reflected in some of the chapters. You may have your own chapters that you could add to this collection. Remember that above all you are hosting a soul that cares for you and wants only the best for you.

The first step to releasing yourself from limitation, fear and illusion, is to recognise that you are bound by these invisible captors. To enable this you must take some time to challenge what you believe about yourself, your world and your reason for being alive at this time. You will find within these pages the guidance to embark on this part of your journey comfortably and safely.

These chapters contain information intended to bring ideas to life within you, which include:
• Possible parallels to your own experiences to let you know you are not alone.
• Simple, yet powerful, exercises to help you untangle the threads that bind you.

- Tips and hints to nudge you along.
- Empowerment affirmations to use repeatedly, until you forget to do them, which is about the time that things have started to shift as a result of your attention to your new life.

When you can 'hear' and decipher your soul messages you will be able to nurture the traits necessary to empower and inspire your passage towards the bliss that your life can be. You will then unfold like a beautiful flower in the warmth of the springtime sun.

You have found this book at the most perfect time. From now on, every day will bring you greater joy, empowerment, love and self-awareness, upon which your inner smile will radiate naturally, to light up your life in the most magical ways. It is an honour to share this part of your journey with you.

Let's get started!

Tree-hugging Optional

Chapter
one

Have you ever known something and felt it to be so true in your heart that when that knowing was involuntarily silenced or left unexpressed a little piece of you withered and was lost?

The opportunity of becoming your own Soul Whisperer is an adventure into the empowerment that is the miracle of **you**. It is all about the journey. Not the **you** who you think you are or the one your friends and family recognise, but it is all about the real **you**. This is the **you** that has a yearning to release the old baggage and stretch your glorious wings that have been tucked away for so long.

You are made up of multiple layers of life experiences, some thicker than others. Strangely, it is the more difficult times in life that many people remember most. The stress, heavy emotions, challenges and pain associated with certain periods in life all leave their footprint on your heart. And then of course there are the people involved, those who you think caused a situation or instigated a difficult time, and the few precious ones who stood by to help you when you needed it most.

Because the happier times resonate with higher emotions, which you might believe are the rewards of life rather than the reality you are meant to permanently live, it is easy to forget about happy occasions.

As humans we need to find meaning in life and it is the challenges that engage us this way, therefore we have a deeper more lasting connection with the more difficult times in our life. It is unlikely that you are going to spend the same amount of time trying to find the meaning behind a fun day out or the happiness you feel.

What if you could flip this emotional paradox on its head? What if your life was consistently filled with the high vibrations of joy, confidence, happiness and a sprinkle of sheer bliss? What if you could transmute the pain, fear, sadness and other uncomfortable emotions into a higher vibration? One that could serve you in a positive way and help increase your inner harmony and heart-connectedness? What would life be like if this was your reality?

If you think that this could only happen to someone else, my question to you would be, 'Why? Why not you?' Your answer might start with, 'Because I am unworthy; I have done some pretty harsh things; I know happiness will always elude me; my partner left me because I wasn't good enough; I don't deserve it; it is beyond me; it's too late for me; that's OK for others; I am different/more wounded/more complicated/unlovable/unsalvageable', and so on.

Whatever your 'reason', it began with a thought. This thought has resulted in a feeling that strengthens it. The original thought and its associated feeling(s) have become so familiar and received repeated reinforcement so that they have eventually become a belief. It is true that we attract what we think about, so if you are putting out any of the messages highlighted in the paragraph above, life will make sure you receive what you are focusing on. You will attract to yourself the kind of people who can 'read', understand and satisfy what you are putting out as a thought or belief about yourself. This is possible because all thoughts are a form of energy. They have a resonance.

Within you is a very sensitive energy receiver, which exists to guide you through your physical sensations. It is one of the forgotten senses that is overlooked, perhaps because it is so subtle or perhaps because we learned to silence its voice long ago. Some receive their messages as gut feelings or experience a definite physical tightening in their stomach.

There are various ways in which the soul delivers its knowing. A soul message can come in the form of body tingles, gut instinct, raised hair and goose-bumps on the arms, itchiness on a specific place on the skin, pressure on the shoulders or head, a tickling sensation on the scalp, a sudden feeling of coolness and/or a sensation of inner warmth rising up the body (different to blushing). These are comforting sensations, and can include feeling as though you are being touched gently by a feather. You may have your own special variety of signals, which are as valid and reliable as those described.

Celebrate these sensory messengers for their gifts because they are there to make you aware of your soul connection. Stop and pay attention to the information or situation during which you get a sensory soul nudge.

Along the way to becoming your own Soul Whisperer, you will start to release some of your layers of limiting beliefs and behaviour patterns. You may find seedlings of forgiveness willing to bud further in your consciousness. Ultimately, as you journey, you will nurture and connect with the deep well of inner wisdom that welcomes this opportunity to infuse every day of your life with its grace, wisdom and guidance.

During the many book promotion events relating to my previous book, *The Soul Whisperer*, I was regularly asked, 'What is a Soul Whisperer?' In my experience, in order to be any kind of whisperer one must first of all be able to connect and listen with an open mind and heart to the voice within. When you can hear the subtle messages from deep within your core you are connecting with the soul.

Next, you need to apply empathic understanding from a place within yourself that embraces great compassion, balance and centredness without ego. I will guide you to easily attain and enhance this knowingness and leave the choice of whether to scale misty mountains, hug the nearest tree or sit cross-legged in silence, while you lose the feeling in your lower legs, entirely up to you!

Tips and hints . . . .

- Take everything at your own comfortable learning pace
- You are discovering new levels of yourself and life at just the right time
- Resist comparing yourself against others or stereotypes
- Remember to take what resonates and leave the rest for another time.

Affirmations . . . .

- I honour my uniqueness every day
- I am ready to explore my inner truth
- I have everything within me to live a joy-filled, loving, abundant life
- I am able to be light-filled, loving and wise.

Voices from a Thousand Lifetimes

Chapter
two

So, to become your own Soul Whisperer, what or who are you listening to? Where did this information come from?

As the name suggests, you are connecting with your soul. So far, so good, however, what and where is the soul? There are many feasible answers to these and other questions such as: Do we all have a soul? What is the difference between the soul and the spirit? Does my soul control my life or do I?

I am all for explanations, yet at the same time, I veer strongly away from getting tangled in semantics and losing the essence of our quest at the very early stages. However, so that you can progress more easily, I will use some space here to give you some information, from my perspective, about the soul.

I apologise to readers of my first book, as we briefly revisit these concepts, however it is essential at this stage.

Please remember that your views and experiences may vary from mine and that's fine. There is no right or wrong, just possibilities. Please always make up your own mind about anything that is presented in my work. In doing so, you will have more faith and belief in your resulting views. When you experience the changes and benefits, they will have more meaning and lasting impact. The positive results you achieve are of your making and in your control. Therefore your growth and journey in life will be richer and more rewarding.

My aim is to give you an opportunity to be more informed, inspired and empowered, through liberating yourself from the fear and illusion that may have caused you pain, stress and unhappiness in the past.

From my understanding, received through various channelled wisdom sessions, research, learning, insights and consultations, the soul is an ethereal energy vibration. The journey of the soul, after healing from its most recent visit to a human host, when considering its next hosting, begins with reflection. Scanning its many past incarnations for the wisdom and learning it has gathered, the soul prepares to continue its quest. During the soul's times between earthly experiences it 'lounges' with other souls who collectively share their gathered knowledge and insights so that all can benefit.

Gradually, with guidance from Source, the soul creates its 'to do list' for the next mission. It carefully chooses the best setting and parents to help it become more enriched during its next visit to the soul school called Earth. I have written in greater detail about this initial connection in *The Soul Whisperer*, if you wish to explore it further.

In general terms, the soul has its own agenda. It is on a continual mission to understand the human condition in all its facets. Ultimately, after hundreds if not thousands of hostings, it returns to the Divine, totally whole and complete, able to serve at a higher level.

The soul energy arrives in the first few weeks of pregnancy. As the embryo takes shape, the heart is the first organ to fully form and function, even before the brain. The soul ignites the heart into life at these very early stages of development by entering the rapidly growing embryo at the union of the occiput, at the base of the skull, and the top of the cervical spine (neck).

This energy surge travels down the rudimentary spinal cord and enters the collection of nerve and muscle cells that have formed the heart, igniting it into action. A short while after birth you start to develop your free will. This most important aspect of being human is unleashed as you start to define your world, experiences and everything about your life. In traditional Chinese medicine, it has long been known that there is a strong energy link between the heart and the small intestine (gut). This helps us understand the signals we receive when we experience the sensation of a gut instinct, which ultimately is your inner knowing sharing its wisdom with you, so you choose the most appropriate action or opportunity. Invariably this will result in receiving confirmation of your appropriate choice through the positive feeling you experience in your heart and you might say, 'It feels right to do this'.

If the soul selects all these requirements for each lifetime, this begs the question, why would a soul choose an unloving family, threatening experiences or extreme challenges? Why would it choose a host that endures terrible circumstances? This can seem a very perplexing situation and unimaginable set of choices. This is because we are trying to find the reason based on our human intelligence. It may not make sense to our human thinking, however, remembering that the soul is being hosted by you means that there is a symbiotic and synergistic relationship in effect. It is the diversity of the soul's experiences that has infused it with infinite wisdom.

This diversity, by its very nature, spans a vast range of experiences and without it you would not be the unique person you are. It is the union of your soul coupled with your experiences in this life that make the journey so varied, rich and expansive. You would be forgiven for thinking that your soul is working against you or that you are the hopeless carrier of some sleeping alien.

The soul knows what experiences it needs to engage with in order to learn and grow. Ultimately, after many hostings it has a full range of understanding through the hosting choices it made to bring it closer to its Divine origins. Your soul brings to you its many lifetimes of wisdom, knowing, talents (that may lie dormant within you), creativity, ability to love and be loved, and a strong connection to Source.

In ancient Egypt, the embalmers honoured the knowledge that the soul resided in the heart and as such, this was the only organ to remain in the body, as a sign of respect for the deceased and to allow the soul to leave when it chose. For centuries, poets, songwriters, mystics and preachers have reinforced the concept that the soul resides in and speaks through the heart, making this a magical and powerful arena for human life, emotion, expression, guidance and wisdom.

Perhaps as modern day evidence of the seniority of the emotions and knowingness, expressed through the soul/ heart, over the intellect of the brain, we should consider individuals, who, as a result of a severe physcial trauma, have no emotional capacity. In tests in which they were required to make decisions, which in their case were based on intellect and logic, they consistently made very poor choices compared with other candidates in similar situations who were capable of using their normal emotions as part of the decision-making process.

In becoming your own Soul Whisperer, you are deepening a connection with a rich source of infinite wisdom. This vast wealth serves to bring to this life the learning and reminders gained in previous human hostings.

The greatest quest of the soul is to know, understand, experience and be fully immersed in unconditional love. In reality, love is all there **is**! In order to satisfy this pursuit, prior to reinstating itself in a new host, the soul reviews its accumulated wisdom and clarifies the next components or experiences that will bring it closer to this understanding.

It is through your experiences, which give rise to resulting feelings, which lead to more solid emotions, that you become aware that you have veered from the best path for you. Once you can hear the whispers, you will be able to recognise when, where and what changes are needed.

It is through the feelings, which gather energy to become emotions, that your health can be influenced. When emotions increase their weight even further they become translated into physical conditions, as proven by the study of metaphysics and psychoneuroimmunology (how the body cells talk to each other in response to strong emotions or thinking patterns). Your soul communicates in the language of feelings. This is how your soul lets you know when you are out of alignment with what is in your highest good.

With this as your underpinning foundation, let's remain with the general concepts to help build a solid foundation for your liberation from fear and illusion and anything else that shadows your happiness and squashes your joy.

You are going to learn how to listen easily to your inner wisdom, awaken and trust your central barometer, and distil the higher perspective for all your life events. Ultimately, in becoming your own Soul Whisperer you will lay your path to greater and deeper joy, love and bliss. You will have the confidence that you are able to discern your heartfelt truth and live in genuine harmony and authenticity. Basically, you will reclaim parts of yourself and your soul that have been lost along the way. You will rejoice in knowing that you are alive at the right time, with your own unique journey and contribution, to create and celebrate.

Your journey will increase your energy vibration as you heal your 'gremlins', thus raising your radiance. By embracing these gifts of grace, you will attract and experience greater unconditional love, in every aspect of your life, starting with yourself. You will recognise that your inner stillness is readily available, that the greatest strength is in silence and that fewer words, well chosen, impart the greatest impact. Thus, my friend, you will be more light-filled, loving and wise. As you give, so you shall receive.

Tips and hints . . . .

- You already carry within you the answers you seek
- You are on a journey of remembering
- Your experiences are opportunities to create a better life.

Affirmations . . . .

- I trust the wisdom I carry within me
- I am aware of the sensations my knowingness/soul sends me
- I listen to my feelings and follow their guidance.

Chapter
three

Do you realise you are a catalyst for change? You have the skills and ability nestled deep within you to touch many people's lives in meaningful and powerfully positive ways.

In the light of my career choices and path, I have often reflected on what prompts one to follow a particular career choice or how we choose to earn our income or express our abilities. I will explain what I understand and perhaps it will shed some light on the vocation or career choices you have made.

It goes like this: healing professionals choose their vocation because they (within themselves) need to heal; touch therapists need to know that touch can be safe and that they can have control over the interaction; teachers teach because they need to learn; law professionals need clear guidelines about right and wrong, order and structure; actors are often multi-faceted individuals in need of recognition, the need to express themselves and be known through the many roles they take on; and so on.

Because life is all about energy, what you think about most, or hold deep within your subconscious, creates the energy and experiences in your life. The Universe, the infinite source of everything, is very literal. It co-ordinates the situations and circumstances that come to you based on what you think about most. As we know, in Universal terms, everything just **is**.

Employing the judgements of right and wrong, large and small, desired or not, is meaningless to a Universe that willingly organises itself to provide what you are thinking about, to bring it into your life. To this infinite source, if you are thinking continually or strongly about something, you must really want it, so there, you have it. You are sent the best (or worst) opportunities to match the energy you are emitting.

Therefore, within your vocation, job or chosen career you are given continual opportunities to receive what you need. A policeperson is continually given the opportunities to clarify (to themselves) the difference between right and wrong by the people and situations they deal with. Therapists and healers attract clients who echo their own experiences. Therefore, as therapists heal themselves, they are equipped to help their clients most effectively, and so on for every role.

I recall during my days of considering being a nurse, then a pharmacist and then a chiropodist, I knew I was in the right arena but couldn't find my proper place in the helping/healing world. Once I explored and cleared these layers, and I discovered what I didn't want, my career path started to unfold and has taken me from being a complementary therapist, healer, teacher and principal, to soul coach, past-life journeywork guide, soul midwife, international lecturer and global soul empowerment specialist. I have seen the changes within me that have led me, through various stages and avenues, to ultimately identify myself as a Soul Whisperer. Without my early experiences, I may never have put myself on this healing journey and become a therapist in the first place. My training and passion to work with others at this magical level, has allowed me to follow my life and soul path. The trick is in knowing when to let go of a 'stage' and move forward with confidence.

It would be easy to think that when you get to a comfortable rung on the ladder of life that you have arrived and there is nothing further to aim for. This is the forerunner of slipping into a deep soul-sleep, where a particular numbness eventually prevails and harvests any scrap of potential, ambition, curiosity, creativity and desire for life improvement. What is left is a shell of the soul-self that just gets up every day, never questions anything and goes about their daily business without distinction from one day to the next. They are on the hamster wheel of life. Are you?

I regularly work with people who are stuck in life, unhappy, dissatisfied, disillusioned and fearful of change. They are often depressed as a result of unknowingly ignoring the soul nudges that were intended to help them grow and move forward. Have you heard the wake-up call from your soul lately? Have coincidences been coming your way only to be brushed aside with a hand wave of disbelief? An awakening is about to happen, are you ready?

Waking up to your world . . . .

From today onwards, take note and keep track of what you think about that soon becomes a reality for you.

If you think about a long lost friend and then within days they call, this is the Universe instigating the opportunity for reuniting both of you.

To wake up fully you must accept that it is OK to make changes. When the path to which you once were committed has fulfilled its purpose and has enriched you to the point where you are ready for a new direction, let your soul give you guidance.

In fact, you may have realised that after you have considered making a change your world starts to respond as though you have already put it in place. In some cases, before you can implement what you are thinking about, your life has benefitted and you are on to the next stage of development. This is further evidence that humanity is ripe for growth and higher consciousness. Just by thinking about making your changes, you will have reaffirmed your commitment to yourself to honour your journey.

The sad thing is that so many people ignore this calling and think that just because they are good at something they have to continue with it. The reality is that they feel honour-bound to remain in the situation even though their heart may no longer be giving that commitment any energy.

The secret is to be alert and listen to the calls from within that reflect around you in the form of new opportunities, interests and coincidences. Change is healthy. Stagnation leads to shut down.

Are you the pebble or the plop? . . . .

When an individual chooses to know more about themselves, make changes, define their boundaries, stand up for themselves and take responsibility for their choices they are like a pebble being dropped into a calm pond. As the pebble, you are a catalyst for change.

The resulting ripples radiate in uniform rings. By comparison, when an individual starts to connect with their soul truth, everything and everybody around them is subtly affected by the ripples of change from that central person. Remember, when you change one thing, you start to change everything around you and this can bring utterly amazing new experiences into your life. Don't worry, you are always in control. Just be open and willing to see your life as limitless and you are half way there.

Eventually, as you can imagine, with all the opportunities for personal and spiritual growth that are available today, these ripples are going to overlap. We are all heading nicely towards this wonderful state, which means that the underlying collective consciousness is rising. In turn, those who have yet to 'wake up' will find themselves in a much more encouraging and comfortable space in which to explore their potential, however, the choice is naturally theirs. They can be the pebble or the plop.

There is a growing global ripple that is making itself increasingly known. This particular ripple started many generations ago with those who knew how to honour their soul's wisdom. They connected with and trusted their intuition. For their livelihoods, wisdom and skills they were outcast, hunted, killed or went underground. This ripple started as a thought, a thought about living life with integrity, authenticity and self-love, in harmony with the magic of nature and one's inner gifts.

What started so many years ago is now playing out more readily in so many ways. It is no longer threatening to explore your inner wisdom, share your talents or gifts, find yourself on courses or retreats designed to give you permission to simply be yourself, and to find out who you are in this process. If you are interested in natural healing, exploring your psychic self and the paranormal it is possible your soul has stored experiences of the challenging times when this was a dangerous life path.

My client and student mix includes many who acknowledge that their current situation is less than they desire. In fact, I tend to view everyone I see as an apprentice because they are seeking learning. This in turn brings their healing through release and illusion diffusion. They also establish a basis from which to build their future life experience. They are ready to make changes and need sound, empathetic and professional guidance from a trusted, experienced resource to be able to release themselves from years of illusion and limitation.

Your soul communicates to you through your feelings and associated physical signs. The heart and the gut are its loudest voices for most people. So, basically, although you may not know the reason why a particular thought or decision feels right, you are receiving your soul's guidance through what is called your intuition and it is your choice whether to follow it.

For now, consider starting your own ripple. Just by seeking greater understanding, awakening your intuition, sharing your gifts and developing your soul consciousness you will positively add to your own and the growing global elevation of human vibration, which is increasing day by day.

The silent dawning of living purposefully, authentically and with joy in your heart will be your signature ripple as you improve the life of others, while yours increases beyond all expectation.

Are you the pebble or the plop? . . . .

If you are the pebble, you will:

- Accept yourself for who you are
- Know that there is no other exactly like you
- Understand that the harmony and perfection of nature always gets it right
- Welcome the opportunity to be catapulted into flight
- Be willing to go head first with everything you have got and grasp every opportunity to create change for yourself
- Proceed with confidence in any situation trusting there will always be a solid foundation on which to rest
- Willingly put yourself in the centre of your world
- Remember that not everyone shines like a diamond, and that is just fine.

If you are the plop, you will:

- Have a brief moment of expression before the cause of your disturbance sinks out of sight
- Be reactive rather than proactive in life
- Wait for someone else to make the first move and then wonder why you never feel in control of your experiences
- Give your 'power' away at the slightest opportunity.

Chapter
four

If you could have three wishes what would they be? And if your wishes were granted, how would you know how to make the most of them?

So often, we dream of what would lead to a better life, relationship, financial situation, career, inner peace, healthier body and so on. Yet, if you have never really experienced what you seek, it is unlikely that you would recognise or know how to sustain it if your wishes were reality. Would you be able to face and accept the changes that might be necessary in order to manifest that which you seek or would you get a bit scared at the first sign of opportunity coming your way? What would your life be like if your deepest wishes were granted?

I have had numerous experiences when life has led me to utter my imploring requests for change and growth in the hope that they would be heard and responded to very quickly. On one occasion, at a time when I had just returned to work after 10 days of reflection and personal growth work, my diary was bursting with appointments for the coming weeks ahead. I was having a good old grumble to the Universe. Although I was grateful for my full diary and career, I proclaimed that I was more than ready to take the next step in my life and would accept the opportunities that would lead to my request being acknowledged. In less than 24 hours I was very unexpectedly in Egypt with a particularly renowned spiritual teacher taking classes on the Nile in a sun-drenched felucca (small Nile sailing boat). I could have easily declined the last place on this final trip with this master, however, having declared that I was ready for my next step in life to be presented, I couldn't decline the opportunity when it was so blatantly presented to me. That trip changed my life and it has led me to many wonderful new experiences and people along the way.

If you are going to ask for guidance, direction, a sign or understanding, make sure you are ready to follow through.

The search for greater life harmony and freedom from the shadows of your past requires you to know your **soul**. This translates as knowing the **S**ecrets **O**f **U**nlimited **L**iving. At the foundations of this knowingness are three tenets that will guide you. Embracing the qualities featured by becoming *light-filled, loving and wise* will open all necessary avenues for an abundantly enriched life.

So what does it mean to be light-filled?

The answer is very simple. To be light-filled means that you naturally and easily radiate from your heart the qualities of graciousness, forgiveness, understanding and unconditional (but not victim-making) love, to the best of your ability, in every situation and with each person you encounter. You are not always going to get it completely right, but the point is that you are conscious and you are willing.

When you are light-filled you are free from the limiting chains of judgement. Being judgemental only serves to bind those who judge into ever constricting mindsets of limitation and isolation. When you create a judgement about someone you lose the ability to ever see them as anything other than what you have deemed. Also, you forfeit the ability to influence them positively in any way. Therefore, a distance is created between you and them that is invisible yet perceivable. In becoming light-filled, although others may have wronged you and made judgements about you, it is possible to forgive without becoming a victim. You can be truly conscious and awake, ensuring you remain tuned-in and switched-on to others around you, yet you provide them with the space to discover that there is another way of being.

To become a 'love' infused person you must first love yourself. With this attribute, the progress towards total connection is all that matters. When we hear that 'love is all you need' it would be easy to think that this is a kind of fluffy, flower-power ideal that has been long forgotten through the decades of war, technological development, politics, crime and disaster. In fact, the greatest prophecy of all time is 'love is all you need'. Terry Loveland (Bowen), my dear friend, psychic medium and fellow soul coach, explains love as **L**oving **O**neself **V**ery **E**asily, and I can wholeheartedly agree with this message.

Love is a power that is involved in every action in the world. Fear is what potentially stops love from manifesting its true power. Therefore, there are only two forces that govern the world and your life: love and fear. Which one will you choose to be your mascot?

To infuse love into your very being, and thus to radiate it genuinely, means that you operate from a basis of accepting yourself first, for who you are, bumps and all.

In so many cases, life is measured by external markers. It is not possessions, position, good looks, designer gear or other temporary attributes that make us lovable. The media pushes ideals that are fantasy just within our grasp, we are told that if only we changed this or became that, all would be paradise.

In reality, you can save yourself a lot of grief, anxiety and money by taking a good long look in the mirror. Just as your eyes are about to translate what they see into a critical voice, catch yourself and make a positive comment about what you see instead. You know that what you focus on you attract, so empower yourself and start to generate feelings that are in your favour.

Touching the soul with love . . . .

A lovely exercise for couples to practise is to sit close together, close your eyes and take turns to gently feel the other's face. Your fingers will sense the person rather than your eyes seeing them. As you do this, ask your inner voice to comment on what is being perceived. Finally, to close the exercise, each place your hand on the other's heart centre. Relax and breathe deeply as you connect with them in this loving way.

From a 'soul knowingness' viewpoint, we know the only thing that matters is unconditional love. This is the root of everything. Most of us are never taught how to love ourselves unconditionally. Instead you went from being a bundle of smiles and gurgles, able to command attention fairly easily with a cry or a bad smell from your nappy, to a mobile force that was constrained and silenced with repeated regularity.

Somewhere between being the adored bundle and the abject teenager seeking loves first encounter, most people seal over the place within their heart where the roots of self-love could have anchored. This is done in favour of finding such validation from others. Ironically, as most other people are in the same boat, it is difficult to find that genuine love because the programme for it remains unwritten within them. Therefore, for some it is fairly impossible to appreciate, recognise or attract real love.

To radiate a loving presence means that you are invincible rather than vulnerable. By connecting with this core soul-self you are sending out the message that judgement, criticism and any other negative pastime, is without fuel and is only a reflection of the sender of these dark energies.

Emanating love reveals those who feel the need to criticise, judge, blame and generally be nasty, very quickly. They are denying their responsibility for creating their own journey towards self-acceptance, inner peace and life fulfilment. So often, when someone has a 'difficult' character it is because they crave the very thing they seem to slander most whether it is love, acceptance or happiness. There may be a severe lack of self-confidence, low self-esteem or limiting beliefs that have formed the basis of their thinking. This results in actions that have provided more fuel to reinforce their thinking about the world and what to expect from it.

Through the processes of becoming light-filled and unconditionally loving there grows an inner core of sanctuary and serenity. Challenges are a thing of the past, as only opportunities exist. Answers come easily as you connect with your inner heartfelt truth. You attract around you those who either already resonate with your vibration or who wish to learn from your example through simply being a friend, lover, partner, child, colleague or acquaintance. All of this generates the final quality of the evolving soul: wisdom.

Many scholars, academics, politicians, public figures and teachers carry vast volumes of knowledge within their magnificent minds and yet the ability to be truly wise may rest within the quiet street sweeper, rarely seen beyond the early hours of day while you are still asleep. The signature of wisdom is the ability to listen with your heart, cast all need for judgement aside as you would only be judging yourself, and then speak a few well chosen words, meaningfully and appropriately, when required.

To be wise, is to honour the needs of another's pathway as they learn through making mistakes, and to lovingly stand by to pick up the pieces if asked. Being wise means that you allow others to be themselves, knowing that your way is just that, your way, and theirs is theirs. Being wise empowers you to always act for your highest good, knowing that the inner sonar of your heart and your gut instincts are more reliable than any spoken word from outside. Being wise is an infusion of life experience, self-understanding, inner peace and harmony with your soul and its purpose.

Embracing the qualities described above means that you are able to be genuine, authentic, compassionate and free from fear, limiting thoughts and beliefs. This is the natural state of your soul, and the distance you are presently from it is shown by how challenging you feel it will be to return to this spiritual homeland. No matter where you are now, it is possible, and you have already started the journey, perhaps without realising it.

If you harbour layers of old 'story' that have convinced you that you are unworthy of a good life, genuine love or that you are unlovable, or that you will never amount to anything, then the journey to know your true self will bring the most magical experiences possible. By retracing your steps in life you will be able to reunite with this most powerful energy force, which is waiting to serve you unreservedly.

With increased inner knowing, acceptance and self-forgiveness, you will feel a sense of well-earned wisdom acting as your backbone. The purpose of wisdom is to guide your own life along its most authentic path. If others wish to tap into it that's fine, but they will need to tread their own path to truly become wise themselves.

For now, as you journey, take each step lightly and let yourself be open to nudges and miracles. There is only the journey and it is at your pace. Release the layers of limitation gradually and you will find a natural sense of becoming light-filled, loving and wise, graciously infuse within you, with one glistening sparkle after another. Are you ready to shine?

Tips and hints . . . .

- Whatever you fear the most about making changes is where your greatest growth lies
- In becoming more authentically 'you' there will be more magic in your life
- Take things slowly, there is plenty of time to enjoy the journey.

Affirmations . . . .

- I have released all shadows of my past story
- I accept change with grace and ease
- I am light-filled, loving and wise every day in every way.

The Dimmer Switch of the Soul

Chapter
five

If you could remember your experiences before you were born into this life, what would they tell you?

In some cases perhaps it is best that we cannot remember. However, there might be some valuable answers and explanations waiting in those distant memories that might help make sense of your life today.

When I take an apprentice on a past-life journey, it is amazing how much detail is revealed. This can help to explain certain present day habits, aptitudes, preferences, fears or traits. If healing is the focus, the journeywork tells me how much is necessary and what amount of past-life release needs to be done. Certainly there are always plenty of new understandings that are absorbed, which can benefit the life path of the client.

On many occasions I have journeyed to the places where souls find respite and sanctuary. To places where the soul receives healing and nurturing so it can consider its continued growth and experience of the human condition. The soul is the infinite spark of energy that infused you with life and a sense of purpose, knowing, guidance and wonder. It can also bring challenges that require delicate translation into meaningfulness.

In most cases, during pregnancy, the growing bump is the subject of great excitement, attention and anticipation. Studies have proved that the foetus can respond to music, sounds, feelings and stimulants. During my years as a complementary therapy practitioner, numerous occasions presented themselves when a pregnant mother-to-be requested treatment of some sort.

Without fail, whether the session was for reflexology, massage or Reiki (energy healing), there were very noticeable responses indicated by the activity of the baby. Often a deep calming was evident. On other occasions, there would be lots of wriggling, jostling and stretching from within before settling down into what seemed to be a very satisfying sleep. The pure receptivity of the growing baby suggested that it is possible that the soothing nature of the therapies touched its soul consciousness. On delivery, most reports suggest that the passage was smooth and without event. Certainly, the temperament of these growing children has been reported as being calm, self-assured and curious about the world, more so than is average in relation to age.

If we understand that the incoming soul carries lifetimes of wisdom, experience and knowingness, it takes a special awareness by the parents to nurture this, while at the same time, educating the child into the ways of the family, culture, society and life in general. It seems that each soul expects to have to go through the basics again and again, adding the special flavouring for the family and situation it has been born into, in order to set about achieving the next stage on its mission.

In some traditional native cultures a new born is welcomed to the planet through a ceremonial covering with red mud. This serves to mark the baby's arrival, let it feel its connection to the earth and to unite its soul/human energy as it transits from its inner world to its outer reality. The red colour of the mud represents the colour of the first chakra or energy wheel spoken of in Ayurvedic eastern traditions. This base chakra is associated with the foundational pillars of a happy, balanced and successful life. They include a safe home, freedom from fear, solid relationships and living your purpose in this life.

In most modern societies there is a lack of honouring the inborn gifts the soul brings, following the initial nine months of pre-birth miracles and magic. Surely it is a miracle in itself that, without too much outside intervention, the baby is formed from two rapidly dividing cells, to a synergy of trillions of cells that orchestrate themselves into a human baby. After the baby has created itself in the watery half-shadowed world of the uterus, the parents 'take over' and start to decide how it can be improved upon, as though it wasn't perfect enough already. Is it not obvious that the baby already knows when it needs feeding, rest, cleaning, loving, playing and so forth and knows how to get what it needs?

Without the need for formal language, possessions or a job title, the baby/soul is shining brightly in its happiness and the simplicity of its life and is there to provide light for others around it. This is what I call the stage when the 'dimmer switch' is fully turned up. However, there are several hands on this switch, all waiting their turn to adjust it to cast only a certain amount of light to meet their needs and expectations.

With each attempt at homogenising a baby into a routine, making it fit into the lifestyle of the family, the dimmer switch gets turned down a few notches. This is not necessarily a problem at this stage, as the baby's light will still shine brightly. However, it is when the next stages of development start to occur that the growing child noticeably starts to lose the ability to shine.

I remember clearly the words of the song *Father and Son* by Yusuf Islam (formerly Cat Stevens), written decades ago, 'From the moment I could talk, I was ordered to listen' and these words sum up the situation for me. Just when we are finding our voice we are silenced. When we start to get mobile, measures are taken to keep us in check. When we start to think freely, we are herded into classrooms and other places where there is an established set of rules and expectations.

By the time a child reaches school age, it is starting to feel the awakening nudges of its inner individuality. Just at that stage, in most cases, the hand on the dimmer switch passes to a stranger, and under the umbrella of education, it is turned down several more notches.

Obviously, it is important to keep a growing child safe, make them aware of the dangers around them and the consequences of their actions. However, it is prudent to remember that there is a wise inner being that is going through the motions of early life, again, as it heads towards fulfilment of its purpose for this lifetime.

Other social encounters and practices all take a turn at conforming and neutralising the soul of the growing person. You might have been brought up in a very strict household or by parents with their own unresolved issues, limiting beliefs and less-than-nurturing behaviours. Perhaps you grew up in an environment that hosted your uniqueness and individuality while giving you consistent yet loving guidelines to help you manoeuvre in this lifetime.

If you feel you have been lulled into a false soul-sleep then now is the time to start awakening. For some, during this enforced Sleeping Beauty state, the soul stirs sufficiently and occasionally 'screams' in an attempt to be heard and released from its entrapment. Have you felt the energy of deep frustration, being misunderstood, feeling misplaced, chronic illness, repeated patterns that consistently bring challenge and further the nightmare?

In other cases, the soul coalesces and can only sigh in resignation at the seeming inevitability of life as it unrewardingly progresses. Underneath there may be a simmering pot of anger, which when stirred only serves to deepen the growing depression within.

Who has their hand on your dimmer switch?

How to ignite your soul light . . . .

- Close your eyes and take a few deep breaths
- Imagine a candle burning steadily in front of you
- This candle has a dimmer switch that is controlled by your sense of self-knowing. How bright is the flame?
- Know that you have control over how big and bright the candle burns
- Think of every positive aspect of yourself and who you are
- Watch the flame get brighter and brighter as you breathe deeply
- Hold that vision as you know it will only get brighter from this day forth
- When you are ready, take a few deep breaths, open your eyes and let a big smile radiate from within
- You have now gained control of your personal dimmer switch. Congratulations – shine as bright as you like.

Chapter
six

What is it about a life event that ultimately determines how it affects you? No doubt you have been through some pretty tough times. Maybe you have repeatedly found yourself in similar unfavourable or regrettable situations.

Perhaps you have started to wonder if this is your lot in life. Wouldn't it be great to know that you can avoid having to go through similar tough times again? How can you break these cycles and be sure that you won't return to them again?

By developing your soulistic consciousness, you will find this essential tool helps ensure that any, and I do mean any, situation can be an instrument for your empowerment and life enrichment. That may seem like a pretty big promise, however, in this and the remaining chapters, I am going to show you how it can be done. Just remember that with the best will in the world, I can only give you the tools. It is up to you to practise how to use them until you become skilful.

The most important skill you need to develop is to learn to view everything with what I call 'soulistic consciousness'. By discovering and practising this mental shift, I have found so many answers. I have been able to take the learning and release the need to repeat the situations that brought the opportunity in the first place. The second most important skill is to remember to apply it.

So what is soulistic consciousness? Soulistic consciousness is the awakening within you of the ability to view *any* event from two distinct yet complementary perspectives.

The first is the human impact perspective. The human impact perspective is the immediate response to a situation or tragedy, whether personal or received second- or third-hand. As humans, it is an automatic response to become emotionally tied in to a situation. By engaging in the situation consciously we satisfy our human need to express the impact of the event through our emotions, thinking and actions. It is part of our humanness that we employ a range of emotions and responses, no matter what the trigger. If we did not, we would be closed to one of the greatest aspects of being alive.

The second is the soul perspective. This involves remaining compassionate while considering the bigger picture from the viewpoint of the unspoken contract of the soul. It looks not only at the good that might come from a situation, but also at the learning, benefits and increased spiritual connection that can be distilled from any given event. It awakens within you an understanding from a higher, more Universal source, which brings to you the possibility of your soul's contracts and agreements made prior to this incarnation. Naturally, the soul perspective arises after the human impact perspective and is an awareness that can take time to become clear.

You may not consciously understand the reason why an event had to happen, however, from a soul perspective, the higher purpose, as carried out by the souls involved, understanding the soul perspective helps move you forward on every level.

In recent years, there have been many major global events both man-made and natural. These have caused us to step outside our regular thinking and the comfort of our daily life and come together to find strength, courage, understanding and healing.

From a human perspective, when faced with a disaster, threat or life-altering event, the automatic response needs to be one of expressing and honouring the thoughts and emotions that are appropriate. This is necessary in order to deal with, and eventually be able to live with or overcome, the event.

From a soul perspective, however, in order to grow, it is really important that you recognise the meaning behind the need for such an event. Depending on the circumstances and how you choose to let them impact you, understanding the soul perspective may take anything from a few moments to a lifetime. Once this is achieved, however, it forms part of the unique tapestry of yourself as you continue to incorporate that learning into your daily life.

The soul knows that it has a responsibility to guide you and to ensure you continue to grow and reach your fullest potential in this lifetime. It is waiting to assist you in ways that you probably couldn't imagine. This is why becoming your own Soul Whisperer will enrich your life so greatly.

The soul knows what it needs to experience. You determine the possibility of that happening, by exercising your **free will**. You determine the outcome of any opportunity, situation and event or decision, by the **choices** you make, based on your desires, expectations, goals, ambitions, beliefs, experiences and influences. Your choices may be closely in alignment to that of your soul's journey, or they may not.

There is a tug-of-war between your soul and your free will. Using your free will you might make a choice that takes you strongly away from your soul path. In doing so, your soul will inevitably gain some helpful insights. By listening to your intuition you will return to your soul path.

A general awakening is happening within our culture and consciousness. Economic, political, social and global events are calling our attention to what really matters in life. The pursuit of **meaning** is more important than ever. This means that the accumulation of possessions or social status is increasingly being viewed as less necessary and in fact more of a burden and block to true happiness. The insatiable quest for power, material goods and accolade has left a trail of broken souls in its wake. In order to recover and ensure you continue to move towards being more authentic, creative, loving and compassionate, it is necessary to learn to accept yourself as the magnificent being you are. In doing so, celebrate your uniqueness, forgive your humanness and know that you are here to learn and journey forth.

You live in a time when global communication brings life events into your home in real time. You are exposed to far greater emotional, political, social, ethical and cultural challenges than any generation previously. However, general coping mechanisms have remained the same. You have the choice of fight or flight. It is time to awaken your soul consciousness and, in doing so, to start to see beyond the events and your instinctive responses and find the true meaning.

For example, you may hear on a daily basis of tragedies that affect individuals, communities or countries through the news network. It is natural to feel sad, worried, grieved, traumatised and angry. These are all very low vibration energies. It is natural to feel these emotions and yet, because these situations are outside of you, all your emotions do is to add energetically to the burden of emotion at the source of the problem.

Everything is energy based and emotions are strong enough to create physical changes within the body. Your low vibration emotions seek to align with, and therefore naturally strengthen, the existing low vibration emotions of a situation and thus enhance that very vibration – so how is that helping?

When we hear of a tragedy, it may involve one specific person or any number, reaching into the thousands. Many unimaginable events have brought the world to a grinding halt within moments of the first awareness. There was no other way to understand what happened at the time, other than from the human impact perspective. In addition, there have been man-made tragedies and natural disasters that have called our attention to the fragility of life and our planet.

It is instinctive that we respond to such events with our human compassion and the need to find the cause. However, as time allows the emotional wounds to begin to heal, this is when the soul perspective can be explored. When tragic events happen, whether involving one or thousands of people, by exploring the soul perspective you will find greater comfort and understanding of the event. You can be more positively influenced by the legacy of soul contracts of the individuals involved.

In the case of a tragedy, it is possible to remain respectful and compassionate towards the individuals affected while considering the soul perspective. Is it feasible that there was a soul contract to make humanity examine itself more closely? In cases where vast numbers of individuals are affected, is it possible that their souls had a contract to be in the same place at the same time, in order to send a greater message across the globe, to remind us how precious life is and what really matters in life? The people involved may each have led their life by their free will to make choices about where to live, work and how they wanted their life to be. Each of those choices throughout their life made sense to them.

While individuals are conducting their life as they feel best, they are actually enriching their life and fulfilling their soul contract at the same time. The key factor here is that decisions are made based on how they feel. The soul resides in the heart, which has a very strong link to the gut, you know about gut instinct and trusting the physical sensations within you when you are trying to make a decision or choose a course of action.

Adopting a soul perspective allows you to remain compassionate, yet brings a great clarity, which diffuses what might have ultimately been the development of very negative emotions, beliefs or repeated behaviour patterns. Employing a soul perspective to a situation means that you free yourself from the limited view that there is always someone else in control and someone to blame, thus creating a victim and a victor.

I have known many clients who are literally addicted to being a victim. This may sound strange, however, this type of behaviour is often based on their underlying subconscious limiting beliefs. These will have been held throughout their life and tell them that they are unworthy of anything better.

For some, staying in challenging situations is better than having to find the courage to break free. It is the comfort of what is known that keeps many trapped in an illusion of what they believe has to be their reality.

Luckily, understanding that it is possible to make significant lasting changes within the beliefs that govern your life indicates that you can start to write your own story and benefit from doing so. You are the pen that writes your story.

Tips and hints . . . .

- Always walk in your consciousness. Take your first step with your human perspective foot, then follow with your soul perspective foot
- Taking a higher perspective allows you to remain compassionate and to be appropriately emotionally available to understand a situation and support others, if necessary.

Affirmations . . . .

- I use my soulistic consciousness every day to benefit my growth
- I am balanced between myself and my soul awareness
- I trust my inner wisdom to guide me.

From Limitation to Liberation

Chapter

seven

The truth is that **any** event in your life can have **only** two outcomes. Either you choose to be **limited** by it or **liberated** by it. You may use different words, however, it all boils down to the same thing. One choice allows you to follow your true path, the other may be a red herring. Those are the choices.

In so many cases, it is easy to choose subconsciously to be limited by a situation and its perceived truths. You may have found yourself getting stuck in the emotional roller coaster and hanging on for the ride.

However, if you are connected to your soul awareness in the ways mentioned earlier, you can choose to take the lesson and release the teacher. In other words, recognise the invaluable learning, no matter how minor or random, and incorporate it into your unique weave that is the tapestry of your soul. In doing so you are building a more intricate, enriched and complete picture of who you are, along with what has made you and your purpose in life.

Perhaps you know someone who pushes your buttons with little or no effort. Do you think they put the buttons there? Did you create the buttons from your own experiences?

If you are questioning this, perhaps take a few minutes and consider the following using your soulistic consciousness. From a human perspective, there is someone (or several others) who know just how to annoy you and set a whole display of emotional fireworks alight. Could it be that you are seeing within them traits that you either have or are capable of within you? Are these the parts of your character and actions that you dislike about yourself? When you see these traits in others you recognise them and your outward annoyance is really a reflection of your inward feeing about yourself.

From a soul perspective, what could these behaviours be trying to show or teach you? Recognising the effects of others on your inner harmony could lead you to understand your effect on others in turn. Consider treating these antagonists with gratitude, even if silently, as you absorb the significance of what they are showing you, so that you may grow still further. When you have done this successfully, you will be amazed how they will no longer fizz on you.

While embodying these qualities, it also means that you are still aware of events around you and that you are alert and perfectly able to live in the real world. Yet you are unavailable for manipulation or disregard. You honour yourself in a way that encourages others to seek your company as they are part of the ripple effect you have created.

Always respond from your own knowingness rather than how you think others expect you to respond. The experience below was just that. Just after Christmas one year, I bumped into a friend who is keen on personal growth. Following the traditional seasonal greetings, I naturally asked how things were going for him. To my surprise, without the need for many words or emotional gravy, he told me that his wife had just left him, taking their young twins with her, and severed the treasured family unit he had so longed for all the years I have known him. My human impact perspective kicked in. 'Oh, I am so sorry. How terrible for you. That is so sad.' I responded as I thought he needed to hear. As I said these words, with good intention, I felt something inside me squirm, telling me that I was not responding in the way I truly wanted to, which would have been more empowering.

With a gentle smile on his face, his words reminded me how easy it is to add to another's situation. 'Be happy for me', he said, 'I am no longer living with an illusion. I can now have more time with my children when we make proper arrangements rather than just kissing them good night. Be glad that I will now have the chance to create a new relationship with someone who truly loves me. Support me with optimism and hope for the future rather than jump into the pit of sadness and add to that energy.'

This encounter shows how easy it is to add to someone's situation simply through instinctive reactions. My friend's viewpoint was from a soul perspective and, while I am sure he went through the range of natural emotions in the first instance, he took a step back, a few deep breaths and connected with the higher awareness that will benefit him and his children for years to come.

If you are wondering how you would respond in a similar situation, think about this – instead of immediately aligning yourself with what you assume is the other person's emotional state, simply and compassionately ask, 'How do you feel about x?' When you have an understanding of their feelings you will have a better idea of how to respond. People who are experiencing difficulty often need others around them to be positive, instead of constantly reminding them of the weight of their situation, which of course only adds to it, causing greater limitation. By offering this approach you are opening the doors for them to move forward in their own way, at their own pace.

It is the choices you make about the events of your life that determine whether your life will be limited by illusion (what you believe to be true) or liberated by the clarity of real truth. It is integral to determining who you are and how your life will unfold. You are the sum of the **choices** you have made arising out of the events of your life.

No one can make you stick in illusion or choose one course of action or another. The choice comes from within you. Others may try to influence you to make a certain decision and, at times, they may present a logical viewpoint that is worth considering. On other occasions, there may seem to be pressure to stay within the limiting belief that is being presented to you by another. In reality, making a choice that pleases another may be the opposite of what you need to liberate yourself and move your life forward or at least bring you greater happiness. By continually meeting their needs, expectations or beliefs, you are kept just where they want you to be – disillusioned and disempowered. No situation is too small in this circumstance.

If you have been through a lot of tough times, it might be easy at this stage to think, 'What's the point?' Rest assured that the relationship between your soul and you (your free will) and your higher self is completely symbiotic and synergistic.

Although your soul may have an agenda, what remains of the soul contract after this lifetime may become part of another journey with another host.

To recognise whether a situation, a relationship, decision or belief is a vehicle of limitation or liberation, ask yourself these questions:

- Does it give me restriction or opportunity?
- Does it generate heavy or lighter emotions within me?

Even better – when you are trying to make a decision, flip a coin. Having decided which outcome is indicated by heads or tails, as this little oracle spins in the air, take note of which side you hope it lands on. In recognising this you have your answer before it hits the floor.

Your answers will give you the truth about anything you are considering.

When you receive a wake-up call it is because you are ready and in need of releasing the illusion of that part of your life. This is by way of preparation for a more enriched journey that you were meant to experience. The alarm clock of your soul is ringing and it is time to wake up to the wondrous person you are. Are you ready to take the next step?

Reality check . . . .

Write down everything you believe about the topics covered below:
- Your childhood
- Your academic ability
- Your creative ability
- Your looks
- Relationship success (with a partner)
- Money
- Happiness
- Health
- About you as a person.

Now, considering each item you have listed, ask yourself these questions:
- Is that really true?
- Who said it was true?
- Why do I believe it to be true?

Now, employ your soulistic consciousness. Challenge yourself to be totally honest with yourself. Don't stop at conditioned thoughts about where a belief came from by saying to yourself, 'That's just the way it is' or 'It has always been that way so it must be true' or 'My parents/teachers/friends/the media say it is so, so it must be true.'

Take time to carefully consider each of the topics you are exploring. It may take a few minutes or a few days. Just be open to knowing that there may be a different reality waiting to share with you.

Having reached a place where you can view your new perspectives, go gently on yourself about the decisions, actions and choices you have made in the past. Without them you would not be at this amazing point of self-discovery.

Treat everything as an opportunity to know yourself better, be inspired, empowered and liberated. Are you a human having a spiritual experience or a soul having a human one? Or are you the weaver, the threads and the tapestry all in one?

Affirmations . . . .

- I embrace my inner wisdom with grace and ease
- I am liberated from limitation
- I am free to make my own choices
- My past serves as my motivation for a better future.

Shoulda, Woulda, Coulda

Chapter *eight*

How many times have you stopped yourself from taking the next step or accepting an offer because even a slight fear has played its ace and reminded you of how badly things might turn out? On the other hand, how recently did you submit to someone's expectations, demands or wishes through fear of the consequences if you did not? I have known both sides of this situation.

No matter what the motivation being offered, you have the choice to never let fear govern your behaviour again. By the time we go through this chapter together, this kind of fear will cease to cast its long lingering shadows, waiting to block-out the light of your next ambition. You have made the last sacrifice of your soul in order to avoid experiencing the same outcome as before.

Fear is simply this **F**alse **E**vidence **A**ppearing **R**eal. Nothing more and nothing less.

'Shoulda, woulda, coulda' is the cry of a chaotic and unhonoured soul, disguising its palpable regret under the term hindsight. It is a sign of someone who fails to learn from their experiences and take control of their choices.

Within you is every tool you need to venture forth in life courageously meeting opportunities and challenges with the same wonderful gusto. When you lament over a lost opportunity, no matter how small and seemingly insignificant, it is a sign that you are possibly resting in a deep soul-sleep.

Alternatively, you may have subdued, sacrificed or even self-sabotaged your wants, needs and desires, in the belief that they are less important than someone else's. You may think you are acting from a place of kindness and love. If this happens occasionally, without any hindsight lamenting, then that is one thing. However, if this haunting song of the soul is a regular emotion-laden feature you experience, then something needs adjusting.

If a perceived fear is blocking your life progress it may have its roots in past experiences you have faced, something you witnessed or were told about, based on another's understanding of a situation and its outcome. For some it may be anchored in a past-life experience.

If this is the case, you might 'know' what is stopping you from making a decision or taking that next step, yet you cannot find the explanation within your experience. Many professionals, particularly therapists and healers, have a strong fear about charging appropriately for their well-trained skills and time spent with a client. On many occasions, I have worked with talented individuals and highly-skilled professionals suffering with this type of fear. Through my soul empowerment approach, it is possible to effectively release the past-life energy tags, which are low vibration 'memories' that can cause a disturbance or restriction in your present life, and which present fears that you have no rational explanation for having or holding.

Common fears are of being harmed or killed for the ability to act as a conduit for healing, using ancient wisdom, practising natural medicine, being cruel while in a position of authority, abusing one's power, being outrageously wealthy or successful and suffering as a result. If you are the subject being controlled by fear, then it is unlikely that you trust your instincts. This is when you can reduce the number of your regretful and disempowering 'shoulda, woulda, coulda' experiences by connecting with your intuition. In addition, there are a few key things to consider.

First of all, if necessary, deal with the practical safety of you and any others involved in your situation. Secondly, assuming that this is dealt with, consider what follows as the starting point on your way to your own empowerment and liberation.

When someone rules by using fear, it is because they themselves are fearful. They may have incredibly low self-esteem, feel desperately unworthy or misunderstood, have experienced an early life of criticism and/or abuse and therefore struggle to feel good enough. For some, this or a similar combination of circumstances turns them inwards. For others, it makes them over-compensate and aim to regain control of their life through wielding fear, as their motivator to gain what they perceive they lost earlier.

Your greatest insight as a Soul Whisperer, is knowing that what these people fear most is being revealed for who they are (or who they fear they aren't, depending on your viewpoint). The most obtuse behaviour stems from the lack of being understood, often through having the basic needs of unconditional love, security or guidance withheld at a crucial time in life. Therefore, perhaps you can see how these individuals could be returned to a place of comfort within themselves. I am not suggesting that you become a therapist to your antagonist, however, remember that it is often our greatest adversaries who make us grow the most. This is the role of a true soul mate.

Just as you would approach a large dog by keeping a safe distance and bending down to their level so as not to appear a threat, consider approaching the person who governs by fear at their level of need. In most cases, what they are seeking is even a small scrap of understanding, recognition and consideration.

When you are governed by fear it strikes a primal cord with your heart. If you conquer that which you fear, there is only love. To conquer the fear, you need to employ love. Most damage to the abilities to give and receive love is caused by fear. When you truly embrace your soul you will be able to recognise and resolve this cycle in your favour. You will also release the need to employ your hindsight so often.

To release yourself from the perceived grip of fear ask yourself this question, 'If the fear I am experiencing was replaced by love instead, how would I feel towards that person/situation/memory/event?' You might be surprised by the answer you get. Fear keeps others at a distance, which for some is the only way they can cope. Love, on the other hand, may imply vulnerability, victimhood and pain. This, of course, reflects the beliefs that you may hold – but are they true?

If you are bound by your own fears, take a few moments to write down what it is you genuinely fear. Then in a mindset of total self-loving honesty ask yourself if these fears are really False Evidence Appearing Real. False evidence can come in the form of beliefs that you have created to keep you safe and free from failure or harm.

In my mentoring work with clients who are stuck in life or their career pursuits, I never find that they are afraid of failure.

Failure is a natural part of life. It is how we learn and improve for the next opportunity. Instead, I repeatedly find that it is the fear of success that stops the forward progress of some very talented individuals. This can come from this life or a previous one, for similar reasons as highlighted previously.

Clearing that belief results in a new determination to succeed and manifest ambitions into reality. It is like walking in a cloud of butterflies – it is so wonderful to experience and witness.

If you are under the influence of spin-off from someone who uses fear to govern your life and/or theirs, take a while to silently observe their behaviour without being judgemental or critical. Ask yourself, what has made them this way? When you have gained some insight, continue observing and ask, 'What positive and appropriate example can I give this person without making me or them seem weak or inferior?'

When you connect with your soul perspective you may find that you receive the answers in your own voice in your mind. This is how your intuition sounds. Go with what you receive, although you might experience some resistance at first. You may discover that the person who rules with fear, simply needs to feel understood, worthy and appreciated. This sends a signal to their psyche that they have nothing to prove and that it is safe to let go of their need to control and manipulate. Above all, wherever there is fear there is an opportunity to nurture calm and understanding. It may not be your role to facilitate this, however, you can gain some insight, thus making sure the experience is of value. Face your fears and see them for the reality checks that they are. Remember that what you think about you attract to you. When you release fear and live in your soul's truth you will hear your heart sing.

Intuition nudges . . . .

Intuition nudges are delivered through:
- Your inner voice, which will sound like your own
- Positive physical responses when your soul rejoices in its truth
- Creative expressions
- Colour choices
- Music that makes you feel alive
- A deep sense of 'knowing'
- The sense of 'rightness' when you trust this inner power to guide you.

Have you Heard your Heart Sing?

Chapter
nine

If love is the greatest quest of the soul and is at the root of our human encounters, then why is it so misused? Why does it cause so much heartache?

Is it because of love's power and potential to control another? Or is it because it is so powerful and desirable that it is used by some as a self-sabotaging weapon rather than an act of self-honouring?

I firmly believe that we all experience our first heartbreak before we can speak. Looking from a human impact awareness level, as a small child you know only the moment by moment reality around you. This is when you truly live in the present. Ask a young child to wait an hour or even five minutes for something and that represents a fairly significant portion of their life. Consequently, for a child to anticipate the return of a parent who has gone shopping without them, represents a very real loss as they only know the present moment and there is no perception of the future. However, as you get older a portion of time becomes a lesser percentage of your life and thus time seems to speed up.

If a child perceives what makes its world safe and happy can be withdrawn for reasons that they do not understand, then they may start to see love as a reward and also as a tool to control and manipulate others. The depth of this belief depends on the quality and consistency of the other experiences the child has from day to day. Because a child is a raw bundle of trusting love, to have this most important pillar of a healthy emotional life corrupted at an early stage rocks the very foundations on which they will base all future relationships, especially the one with themselves.

Behaviour patterns such as: acting out to gain attention; becoming a victim to secure what they think is love; always looking for reassurance; suffering mental, physical, emotional and sexual abuse; can all arise out of the lack of self-esteem and disempowerment brought about by the fear of being unloved, rejected and abandoned again.

Children's emotions are as significant as those of adults. In fact, until they develop some reasoning ability, emotions form the greatest part of their vocabulary. These youngsters have yet to learn how to understand what they are experiencing in these events, so until then they are more easily wounded. This is what starts to form the thinking and beliefs from which they will make choices in later life.

How many times have you heard a frustrated adult say to a disobedient child that they are going to leave them as they start to walk away, in an attempt to encourage them to hurry up and follow? This threat of being left behind may seem like a good motivational tactic, however, to the child it strikes the primal fear of being abandoned. The trust you have in others and ultimately in yourself is largely based on the security you have experienced in the past. All kinds of thoughts can arise in a child's mind based on what they experience and the meaning they give it. In so many cases, the perception of being loved, and indeed lovable, is muddled with good behaviour, achieving the right school grades and securing a solid career.

Do you think you have been limited or liberated by the standards that were put in front of you as the conditions for acceptability and love in your parents' eyes? These standards might have sounded something like this: 'Eat all your food and you will be a good girl/boy', 'Study hard and you will get a good job', 'With a good job you will have a nice home and attract a perfect spouse', 'Work hard at your job and one day you can retire', 'When you retire you can be happy and do what you like'.

Ask yourself this, did those standards and expectations work for the people who said them? Are they really happy in their work, living the life of their dreams, comfortable in a long term relationship that has strengthened as it endured the rough times? Do they know what it feels like to hear their heart sing in confirmation of experiencing a life of joy?

Admittedly, you would expect parents to want the best for their children and they are only passing on the guidance that they themselves received or they thought would have made their life better. However, either way, you are being encouraged to live by a formula that to date has produced the highest number of divorces, greatest ever volume of prescriptions for anxiety and depression, a boom in self-help approaches, mental health support centres, millions of therapists trained to sort out your mind, body and soul, and thousands of opportunities to tap into self-help talks, books, programmes, workshops and schemes.

Why not turn it on its head? How about doing what makes you happy, makes your heart sing and follow your intuition as it guides you to the great partner, to find the type of work that inspires you towards a career that challenges you just enough to express your inner creativity and gifts, and save the hard work for thinking how best to increase your fun factor in life? So where does the heart singing come in? In truth, it should be within every fibre, cell and breath that makes you who you are. This is parallel to the feeling of having a golden glistening thread that acts not only as an anchor to keep you steady and stable, but also that ties you to a beautiful balloon that lets you float carefree in a cloudless sky on a perfect summer's day.

Many people experience love as an uncertain and sometimes insidious game, in which they are led to think they are treasured and important, until the illusion is withdrawn, without valid explanation. In these instances, love and its subsequent withdrawal becomes a very powerful tool for the dominant person.

A child exposed to such behaviour learns quickly to mistrust what is presented as love. They may become a victim to please another, may suffer humiliation or be vulnerable for the sake of trying to find a steady level of the love they seek. All these experiences are the consequence of the perpetrator, usually an adult and/or parent, expressing what they themselves have experienced or need to make them feel less of a victim. This is when the heart is heavy with sadness.

When this is translated into an adult relationship, the weaker person languishes and stokes the fire of their partnership through the fear of being rejected (again), which serves to feed the hunger of the other person. I have known of so many instances when a confident, self-assured person enters a relationship with someone who seems equally self-confident only to find that, through a subtle constructive withering, one of the partners, ultimately consciously or not, dissolves the other into a submissive lapdog grateful for any crumb of attention and affection.

These situations are also a result of fear. It could be the fears held by one or both of the people involved. This is the fear of rejection, abandonment, being unloved, alone, getting it wrong again, being unwanted, useless or anything else that sticks like chewing gum on the sole of your shoe. Thankfully, not all relationships mirror these scenarios. However, it is very possible that at some point in your life you have had some experience in this arena, which may continue to resonate within the scars on your heart.

In some cases this may be the only way someone can show what they think is love. From a human perspective, you may resonate with some of these conditions, perhaps you could add to the list, and you are well aware of the scars you carry as a result. These scars are like the signatures of the person who gave you the experience or thoughts that have become your beliefs about how lovable or loved you are. It is time to let these old voices be silenced once and for all. It is time to let the deep healing begin. It is possible to let your heart sing again no matter what your past has entailed.

To start with let's take the soul perspective on the above. Remembering that the soul's greatest quest is to experience love on every level and in its many forms, it is possible to start to view the love experiences that have left you alone, hurt, questioning and vowing never to go down that route again, with a more life enhancing view.

For every sad or unsatisfactory experience you have had, consider that one of these truths may be the reality you were part of:
• Your soul agreed to have the experience in order to help itself and you grow in the best way possible ready for

better experiences in the future.

- Your soul agreed to facilitate the experience in order to help the other person(s) involved learn something that will enrich their growth (and that of those in their life) if not immediately then later on.
- Your soul knew that the situation was off track with your highest good in this life and therefore ignited your inner wisdom through your heart/gut feelings to get you back on track.
- Your soul had some karma (cause and effect) to repay and this opportunity gave the chance to redress the balance by understanding a different viewpoint for your own growth.

So how do you know which one is correct? There is a way, but first of all ask yourself how important it is to know the reason? If you know the reason, from a soul perspective, are you going to incorporate that into your understanding of yourself and life and use it to make things better? Or are you just going to find some way to hurt yourself or another with that information?

If you are willing to use this wisdom to enhance your life then try this. Sit quietly, breathing slowly and deeply. Use all your senses and imagine a situation in the past where you felt really happy, carefree, full of joy, blissful and when life was totally as you would like it to be.

Really sense these emotions as you hold your hands to your heart. You are connecting with the hero in your heart, the intuitive messenger who makes your heart sing.

Breathe deeply. Feel the exhilaration rising in your heart. It may gently race a bit or flutter in response to the wondrous emotional uplift. Once you have a firm recognition of what I call the heart-sing feeling return to a normal breathing pattern as you clear your mind.

The philosophy behind the heart-sing feeling is that your soul knows the truth and it communicates it through your feelings. This is another way your intuition speaks to you. When you really connect it translates its message, through your emotions, because you will hold the feeling long enough to generate specific neural messengers that transport the emotion, in chemical form, throughout the body, and in this case deliver them to the heart.

With your hands to your heart, in each circumstance below, take time to register whether your heart sings, sighs or screams. Think about different aspects of your life. Consider your relationship, occupation, health, how you treat yourself, how you conduct yourself, how you treat your family/friends/work colleagues/shop assistants/slow drivers/loud teenagers/people who dawdle in front of you and any other part of your life that has an impact. Take a few moments in between each to register any sensations arising in your heart. Without forcing it, try to sense which one makes your heart sing.

So, with a bit of practice you will be able to understand whether these areas of your life are true for your soul. You will begin to realise which areas need adjustment. You can employ this technique with any situation, thought, belief or question you are trying to answer. You will always receive the response that is best for your highest good.

Now that you have an answer what are you going to do with it? This is the place where the human and soul perspectives do a dance. In order to fix a part of your life, start with the human perspective. Without judgement or criticism, look at the impact and the resulting thoughts, beliefs and actions so that you can start to awaken your WOW.

Affirmations to allow your heart to sing . . . .

Work with these until your heart tells you to stop:
- I am free from limiting emotions
- I have released all anger
- I live in my truth every day
- I attract only nurturing experiences
- My joy increases every day
- I breathe in happiness and breathe out sadness/pain/disappointment/etc.

Chapter

ten

What would it be like to change your hamster wheel of life, full of limiting beliefs and fear, into a rewarding and exciting path you could follow easily?

Can you imagine easily and effortlessly trading a cycle of continual restriction, frustration, and endless running to get nowhere, for one that is full of choice, opportunity and abundance?

Nestled within you, increasingly revealed every day is your personal **Weaver Of Wisdom**. This weaver is a skilful master who, along with your soul, creates the most majestic and awe-inspiring tapestry of your life.

Your WOW is your higher self. It is the embodiment of you in this life when you are at your zenith of being yourself. You are in your groove, standing on a mountain top, your senses alive, arms outstretched to take in all you see and be part of the majesty. The feeling of living as your higher self is basically you on the best day of your life ever, always. This is confirmed by feeling your heart sing. It is when everything is going right and you want time to stop so nothing ever changes. It is your soul dancing the dance of life without caring who is watching.

When your soul and your higher self join forces, life becomes pure bliss. Your higher self can only achieve its expression through living your soul's truth, which naturally means that you are drawing on wisdom and experiencing your heart sing in confirmation.

Imagine that every thought, feeling, emotion, belief, action, personal preference, memory, relationship, occasion and person you have ever met is an individual thread. Each of these threads has its own colour, texture, particular character, vulnerability and strength. Left randomly unattended these threads would easily get disorganised and/or become knotted and tangled by the movements of everyday life. Your WOW is fuelled by the sequential and continual evolution of yourself towards the most empowered and vibrant person you can be. It is the sum total of all your positive realities. It is real, makes you feel alive and can grow in an instant.

Your soul is your guardian to your Weaver of Wisdom. The weaver's key role is to treat each thread as an invaluable part of the tapestry that represents you and your life. Like your life, the picture unfolds one thread at a time. Connecting with and embodying your higher self can happen at any time as the picture becomes recognisable. It may initially be a regularly fleeting experience before becoming more permanent. Although this means that until the final shuttle has come to rest, the journey of your life hangs on the loom of time, you can start living every day in this wondrous state, before your tapestry of life is fully complete.

As you know, your soul operates on the language of feelings, which gives rise to your intuition. This tangible physical response to opportunities, questions, challenges and decisions guides you towards living as your higher self. So often, when faced with a decision, your internal dimmer switch, the light your soul hosts, is turned down so low that you are unable to register the messages your soul is trying to deliver through your intuition. Instead, whatever does manage to sneak through into your awareness is quickly silenced in favour of the chatter your head produces. It would be such a crime against the soul if the representation of your life was made up of chaotic, random and dull threads, none of which related to the other in any discernable way. For some, however, this is reflected through their journey in this life because their higher self is truly un-honoured.

Five keys to unlock your WOW . . . .

Your Weaver of Wisdom requires a simple diet to keep it alive and growing so that it may best serve you. However, as with any diet, is it the quality and quantity of 'food' that makes the difference between a vitally alive and unstoppable person and a couch potato.

1. Thoughts
Thoughts feed on your experiences and how you choose to interpret them. In doing so they are validated. Thoughts start to separate you from the reality of the situation. In many cases, when assumptions are made, conclusions are drawn and further thoughts are generated, which, in turn, fuel more thoughts and so on. This spiral of interpretation can lead to some amazing or disastrous outcomes.

In response to your thoughts you create a feeling. This can happen almost instantly, to the point where you might not recognise the distinction between this and an emotion.

2. Feelings
Feelings are your polygraph to determine what is in accordance with your highest good. This is what brings you closer to feeling permanently light-filled, loving and wise. As Denise Linn, the founder of Soul Coaching says, 'The soul loves the truth.' When you are in your truth, I call this the mountain top feeling, your higher self feels limitless and the world is open and available, revealing all its beauty, which echoes what is

inside you already. When your feelings are non-judgemental, it gives you the opportunity to test out possible decisions or outcomes before you make an all important choice.

From your initial thoughts about something, you create your feeling's response, in order to give the topic some weight and meaning.

The feeling process seeks validation from all contributors around it. From this initial stage, inevitably, as the feelings persist, the hard-wiring of emotions occurs. It is at this stage that the effect of the initial thought that led to the feelings becomes more powerful as it becomes an emotion. It is when the voices of others, who perhaps instigated your feeling response, gather volume, and your free will to choose between the validity and accuracy of their words is lost to you. By now, your inner voice has been virtually silenced, perhaps only to be heard in the future as a frustrated 'soul scream', voiced through physical or mental ill-health when you are really in need of bringing back on track.

3. Emotions

Emotions power your actions. Emotions cause physical responses both inwardly and outwardly. Emotions are pure Energy in Motion (E-Motion). However, en route to this outcome, crystallization happens. Emotions release chemicals, which can be addictive as they ignite the body into physical and emotional responses. Adrenaline triggers fight or flight responses, oxytocin fuels the thrill of new love, and the stimulus of the solar plexus behind your stomach gives you the feeling of butterflies in your tummy as you anticipate a challenge. Some people choose to live continually by experiencing physical messengers triggered by their emotions. You might know someone who is a perpetual worrier, drama queen or thrives on stress and catastrophe.

Emotions serve to validate your feelings and consequently your thoughts. This in turn creates an internal measure that reflects your beliefs about yourself, your place in the world and how you experience life around you.

4. Beliefs

Beliefs can either serve or destroy. They can hold you together or tear you apart. They can be liberating or limiting.

Beliefs generate further emotions to reinforce their anchoring within you. This endless fuel will always find its source, as what we seek will always be attracted to us and come like a magnet to satisfy our desire.

It is from your beliefs that your actions are generated. Rational or not, in your best interest of not, in alignment with your soul purpose or not, your beliefs always govern what happens next. That's the reality.

5. Actions

Actions bring what was initially within you as a thought, to the outer reality. They make permanent and memorable your thoughts, feelings, emotions and beliefs. They are available as part of your tapestry for others to experience.

Finally, just as a spiral working its way to the iridescent pearl within you, after actions come more thoughts. Through applying your skills as a Soul Whisperer you awaken and honour your WOW through reflection and honestly recognising your soul's truth. As you honour your higher self, your self-confidence, relationships, career, health, life success, wealth, abundance, happiness, joy and 'luck' all benefit. The ultimate fulfilment of your life and soul purpose all begins with a thought. It is here that you must remember that if you change one thing in your life, others things will change as a result. You will be creating and living your ripple, which can be pretty amazing journey and well worth it.

Connecting with your WOW . . . .

Have you ever experienced that 'mountain top' feeling? When you stand face to face with the world and are inspired and enriched just being there. Connecting with your Weaver of Wisdom is a liberating and empowering experience. It gives you an invaluable opportunity to continually view and review your thoughts, feelings, emotions, beliefs and actions, which can, in turn, positively influence your choices, decisions and future responses. It only fails if you are less than completely honest with yourself. On the basis that you are reading this book, I assume you are ready to rock in relation to all you can be.

You are opening yourself to your higher wisdom and awakening the weaver in you. You are being given the opportunity to exercise your soulistic consciousness. You are increasingly open to arrive at the awareness that if x hadn't happened, you would have missed the opportunity to be aware of y and so on. The dawning of your higher self can illuminate every step of your path by helping you move beyond just being satisfied with finding the good in a situation.

Understanding your higher self creates a harmony between what your soul seeks to understand and the choices you make in life.

This synergy ideally brings to you what is necessary for you to move forward as a more empowered, complete person, free from limitation and illusion. It puts you 'in your groove'.

The answers are there waiting to be delivered. The feelings you experience arise from your soul and this is the resource that offers the answers. When you are familiar with the method of delivery, you are further along the path to becoming your own Soul Whisperer. Make sure you honour everything that you receive. Avoid dismissing a message because it is in your own voice, too simple, too far-fetched, too obvious or too good to be true.

Let your soul and higher self guide you and resist the temptation to analyse or question the feasibility of what you have received. Remember, everything just **is**. It is your humanness that seeks meaning, answers, control, logic, and convincing, which is derived from fear. Let yourself be on that mountain top always.

Eleven easy steps to awaken your WOW . . . .

1. This can be a visual or pen and paper exercise. Choose a challenging event or episode from your life. Thinking backwards from the end result to the initial motivational thoughts, spend some time just focusing on this event so you get a clear picture and raise the juices of the memories.

2. Explore the **actions** you displayed. Would they enhance your mountain top feeling?

3. What were the **beliefs** that fuelled your actions? Where do they come from? Who instigated that belief?

4. You can probably feel the **emotions** surging through you by now, so write them down as well. Be clear and non-judgemental. If you feel downright angry – say so. Be totally honest with yourself. Nobody else will see what you have written – go for it!

5. What were the initial **feelings** that were so strong in you that they caused you to take things further? Fear, excitement, challenge, happiness, frustration, lack of confidence, acceptance, being understood or acknowledged, deflation, injustice, dishonour, disgrace, embarrassment, love (or some definition of it as it was put to you), joy, bliss, shame, rejection, abandonment, or something else?

6. Recall and record what **thoughts** you carried in the initial stages of this experience. In other words, what started this episode in your life? Where did these thoughts come from?

7. Now, sit in stillness and quieten your mind. Breathe deeply and centre yourself.

8. Next, ask yourself, in relation to the situation you are considering, did you act in accordance with your true higher self or as a result of the voices, beliefs and perhaps the expectations of others? Chances are that you will recognise that you were acting outside your soul's comfort zone. This is very often the case when the dimmer switch of the soul is turned down because it is more difficult to define and connect with the true you that you were born to be.

9. Having recognised where you veered from honouring your higher self, replay the situation in your mind through the voice and sensation of being your higher self. Take a few deep breaths, connect with your mountain top feeling and start by addressing your **thoughts and feelings** about this situation, at your core. When you have connected with your truth, there will be a sensation in your heart or gut. By changing your initial thoughts you start to change everything. Let these feelings grow into new **emotions**. Your inner resources will guide you as you develop this vocabulary to its fullest extent.

10. Examine what **beliefs** would be different in the light of this exercise. When you recognise your true beliefs, would your actions have been different? You can now use what you have just learned to enrich your life using this process of awareness.

11. Finally, acting as your Weaver of Wisdom, return to the present moment, note down the differences between the past situation and the one you just witnessed. Note how your thoughts, feelings, emotions and beliefs have shifted. Most importantly, how will your new awareness of your higher self positively influence your future?

You can use this invaluable process for any situation, past or present, and even for answering the perpetual question of 'what if?' Your soul loves the truth and your higher self makes sure you listen to it. In getting to know your underpinning hard-wiring you are able to dissolve and resolve old patterns. Now you know how to turn up your dimmer switch and shine in your own unique light.

Wasting time beating yourself up for things in the past only serves to add bruises to an already wounded situation. Start your own healing by gently honouring that everything has learning within it.

Celebrate your journey and newly awakened WOW. In doing so, you will be enriched by taking the lesson and removing the need to repeat the learning process for that life-lesson. You have taken a leap forward in your growth. Proceed confidently and know that the path unfolds before you one step at a time. Your higher self is the radiant, magical, miracle maker that makes you feel alive every day.

Tips and hints . . . .

- Take your time over the above exercise
- Go gently with yourself on the bigger issues
- Remember that every event has meaning and has helped you grow.

Affirmations . . . .

- My life unfolds perfectly
- Life supports me in everything I do
- I trust my inner wisdom
- I honour my Weaver of Wisdom/higher self every day.

Chapter
eleven

Declaring yourself IN!

Do you remember which character, fictional or not, with whom you most identified during your childhood? Was it a superhero or a Disney character? What were their qualities?

It is said that A A Milne based his characters in the Winnie the Pooh stories on the basic personality archetypes most commonly found in society. Are you a Tigger, Piglet, Owl, Eeyore or one of the other characters?

The attributes of your character are the qualities about yourself that you are aware of and operate by or you desire to make part of yourself.

'Declaring yourself in' means stepping up and letting yourself be 'seen'. It means you know yourself, your strengths, your weaknesses, desires, and abilities, well enough to be able to recognise and accept new opportunities that help enrich the tapestry of your life.

In growing into the person you know yourself to be, there needs to be a foundation on which to build. Perhaps your childhood nurtured and supported your individuality, creativity, self knowing and recognised your qualities. This would most likely mean that you have always had plenty of confidence, self-reliance and belief in yourself, which is absolutely great if that is your reality. It also means that you have got this far in this book and may be thinking of a friend or two who could benefit. Pass it on when you are done, with my blessing.

However, for most of us, the story of our life contains many interesting chapters and tells of experiences that have formed us into someone different and distant from the one we were born to be. In other words, when you were a new born baby, your soul was guiding you to navigate the early years when you could not communicate verbally to have your needs met. In those very early years, while your personality was defining itself and trying out its features to gauge their effectiveness, at the same time you were also being honed into the family unit, for better or worse.

They say that children should come with an owner's manual, which is a fair comment considering the mammoth task for new parents. Equally though, I feel it would be helpful for children to have a textbook of some sort to help them better understand their parents. As children we tend to forget that our parents were people before they had us, and that they had a life with a vast range of experiences that made them who they are.

Knowing more about what hard-wired your parents, would help to demystify and detoxify some of the behaviours, attitudes and beliefs you might have experienced or taken on as you grew up. So often, fears, feelings of inadequacy, a history of poor parenting, unresolved emotional pain, and difficult life experiences become an entangled mesh of beliefs and behaviour patterns. These are triggered by the offspring as they inadvertently push a button or two without realising that there was a significant degree of emotional baggage waiting to be unleashed.

In cases where your parents, or the significant adults in your life, have consistently offered the experience of increasingly difficult and sometimes irrational behaviour, ruling by fear, manipulation, sharp cutting words, criticism, shouting or occasional force, there may be several underlying factors fuelling this string of undesirable traits. If you have experience of a delicate or overly sensitive parent whose behaviour you find disempowering, making you feel out of balance, uncomfortable and cringe-worthy, before judging them too harshly, ask yourself what have they been missing in their life to make them this way?

Nobody is born with such deep inexplicable unhappiness. The reality is that the soul is characterless, it just **is**. People make people, in every way possible.

If your 'difficult' person fits somewhere on the 'toxic scale' there is a reason for their behaviour. It could be from jealously and feelings of inadequacy when a new child enters the family. They may interpret the resulting attention the newborn receives as a rejection or even abandonment of themselves. This can lead to a myriad of attention seeking behaviours, which sadly may become ingrained and become their character expression as they grow older.

It may be that they were brought up in a time that saw children as little adults who were seen and not heard and thus a creative, expressive child would have become very familiar with feeling frustrated, creatively squashed, insignificant and unimportant. The emotional development of a child requires a rich and delicate blend of stimulation, guidance and nurturing to allow the innate qualities of mind, emotions and soul to fuse together to form the authentic self-honouring person they were born to be.

In these situations, you are the only person who is being affected by this emotional legacy. The others involved may never have realised their impact, even if they are still in your life today.

You are the sum total of your choices. Your continuing experiences serve to provide you with the opportunity to make new choices about the meaning, effect or outcome of any situation. Blaming another for what they have 'done' to you is fruitless. It is you who decides what has been done to you. When you employ your developing Soul Whisperer abilities, you will initially engage with the very human emotions of justice, fairness, right and wrong, victimisation and anger. Fine, go for it! Get it out of your system, the faster the better. Then when you can take a step back, employ your higher sense of your soul perspective and work towards experiencing your higher self.

Ask yourself what your choices are about responding to this memory, belief, incident or event. Consider what message may be in the motive behind the action you witnessed or experienced. What if that situation was orchestrated specifically for you to learn something that will be of great value either now or in the future? If you find yourself repeating a similar situation from the past, look at what the hidden messages and meaning might be and in doing so you will release yourself from the need to repeat the event or learning opportunity again.

From the soul perspective, when you look at the bigger picture, you will find that as the threads that weave the picture come together, you are able to take a metaphorical view and become the witness to your life being enriched by the realisation of the information your soul is delivering.

Declare yourself in by . . . .

- Defining yourself only in positive terms
- Surrounding yourself with like-minded people
- Putting all Soul Whisperer skills to their fullest use
- Viewing your life experiences with the gift of wisdom rather than blame and judgement
- Honestly and realistically acknowledging what influences have positively and negatively left their imprint
- Dealing with less-than-positive experiences with fairness to all concerned, remembering that others are also on their journey, whether they realise it or not. Allow them to travel their own path in their own way unless they seek guidance
- Accepting challenge as a positive opportunity to be creative
- Incorporating all the lessons brought your way with grace and ease, knowing that it is how you choose to respond to an event that makes a lasting impression.

Undeniably by taking the time and insight to define yourself, you can declare yourself truly in line for the wonders of your life. Through this you will form a deep sense of self-esteem, self-respect, confidence and clarity about who you are. In doing so you are able to create healthier relationships with friends, loved ones, your partner and especially yourself.

Remember, past hurts pull you down. Declare yourself to be free from these wounds. You hold the key to unlock the door to the future of your dreams. Start now to define your tomorrow. Step into your true knowingness of yourself and you will radiate a totally different energy. This naturally means that you are going to attract people and experiences that mirror what you are sending out. Get ready to radiate and light up your world with your Weaver of Wisdom. So, are you in or out?

Affirmations ....

- I release all unfounded fear
- I am worthy of being loved
- I am lovable
- I am love
- I live each day with radiance
- I am confident
- My self-esteem guides me accurately to experience only what is in my best interest.

The Art of Self-honouring

Chapter
twelve

During my life I have known many forms of abuse. Do I consider myself a victim? Am I a less worthy person to enjoy happiness? Am I dirty? Am I guilty of attracting these experiences? Do I use this as an excuse when life gets rough? The truth is that for many years I would have answered 'Yes' to all of those questions.

Mental, emotional, spiritual, sexual and physical abuse all carry scars that affect every level of one's being. Above all, any uninvited crossing of boundaries is a violation of the soul. When your instinctive and personal boundaries are crossed without your permission you are experiencing abuse, whether it is a family member who conveniently sends their spouse to find something as they impart a lingering goodbye kiss, repeated emotional blackmail, or enduring guilt and fear. These kinds of wounds resonate much, much deeper and longer than any physical bruise.

In terms of human self-perception, victims often blame themselves, and this, in turn, starts to eat away at their self-respect, confidence and esteem, and creates the belief that this is how their life is going to be and this is what they deserve. Expecting nothing better, behaviour and resulting encounters further reinforce this growing belief until an emotional apocalypse occurs. People who have been abused often continue to self-harm through food, alcohol, workaholic tendencies or other means of escapism.

For women, the most common route is through food, either through denying oneself or by overindulging to create a pronounced layer of protective fat around the lower abdomen, symbolically protecting the reproductive and sexual region. This lipid shield makes the person feel less attractive and therefore less likely to be a victim again. However, they become victims and prisoners to themselves.

As a consequence, the idea that they are unlovable, unworthy of genuine affection and unwanted is reinforced. In these cases, sexual desire, creativity and feelings of self-worth and self-respect are all 'safely' buried far from reach and thus far from being part of an empowered life. Ultimately, these feelings may gather enough energy to create one of several common illnesses and diseases of the reproductive system. If you feel this may be relevant to you, you are not alone. A significant number of my private consultations and workshops focus on the metaphysics (mind–body connection), during which the tools of empowerment are discovered through soul awakening to resolve the need to break this pattern.

From a soul perspective, by taking a step back, it is possible and valuable to consider what made the abuser into such a person. It is so often the case that, not only is there a history of this type of behaviour within the family, but often the perpetrator is acting out the only way they know of experiencing what they consider to be love and closeness.

In addressing this most delicate situation, please understand that I am in no way condoning or excusing this type of behaviour. At least, if you know something about the perpetrator's upbringing and background it may help you to understand from where they received their influences, issues and baggage. If you have found yourself on the receiving end of some form of abuse, now is the time to ask yourself, how is that serving you in your life today? Is it an excuse that keeps you 'safely' isolated, disconnected and less vulnerable? Does it block your relationships? Does it halt your ability to get close to or enjoy being intimate with a genuinely loving partner? Does it make you hold back in showing affection to your children?

Bizarrely, I have known situations in which a history of abuse has been turned into a very handy 'reason' why relationships never work out, why there is no point in trying to find a good partner and so on. The route to self-honouring releases the self-saboteur and the self-critic.

However, as ever, you have a choice. You can either hold on to the anger, resentment, victimisation, low self opinion and so on, or you can take the learning and live your truth. This turns the effects of the event(s) into something more positive, powerful and longer lasting. Therefore, you can choose to take the view of an empowered person and declare yourself free from the need to remain in the victim mindset and release the re-occurrence of self-sabotage. For some people, self-sabotage is the act, or art, of consciously or subconsciously destroying the potential for their dreams, ambitions, desires, relationships and even their path in life from manifesting. For many, it keeps them safe and in their 'story.' Others see it as an act of duty to the situation they have created around them. Either way, self-sabotage is a one-way street leading nowhere.

To release yourself from whatever binds you, and the other parties concerned, takes understanding and a willingness to own your reality. One of the best ways to achieve this is to energetically cut the cords to the individual or the event, preferably both. This is the starting of forgiveness. As I wrote in *The Soul Whisperer*, forgiving allows the negative energy to dissolve, leaving you free to harness that energy for your own life-enriching use. It means that you can let go of the need to stay trapped in an old memory. It means that you are infused with your sense of self, without the chance of attracting or accepting the behaviour or welcoming the same again.

Exercise for cutting the attachment . . . .

This simple exercise can be done as a visual journey while sitting quietly with your eyes closed or as a pen and paper exercise. This exercise has freed thousands of people from the energy that binds them, now it is your turn.

Relax, take a few deep breaths and get yourself centred and comfortable.

Imagine the person who you wish to release from your energy memory standing a safe distance in front of you. You are in control. Imagine there is a golden cord extending from your solar plexus (just at the central base of your rib cage) to theirs. Along this cord you are going to communicate by speaking in your mind's voice, or writing if you choose, anything you have ever wanted to say to them. Know that your message will be heard and understood, so really go for it. Ask any questions to which you need an answer and allow the response to come.

When the exchange is complete to your satisfaction, it is time to cut the cord and release them from your energy. When you do this you are releasing yourself from their influence on you. No physical harm will come to either of you.

As you cut the cord, say to yourself, write it or say aloud, 'I release you from my energy. Go in peace. I forgive your actions and set you free. And so it is.' Finally, and most importantly, call a reflection of yourself to stand in front of you. Extend the golden cord and offer to forgive yourself for anything for which you hold yourself in negative energy. See and feel the release as you cut the cord and say, 'I set myself free. And so it is.'

You may need to repeat this exercise calling different individuals into the frame. The process is the same for each situation. If you have done this exercise using pen and paper, when you have finished, carefully burn what you have written as you are then liberating yourself in a very positive and lasting way.

When you empower yourself in this way, you will find that you have a tremendous amount of energy newly available to channel into other areas of your life. Allow yourself to grow graciously into this new awareness and you will find more beauty where once there was shadow in your life. This is a major step towards hearing your heart sing and connecting with your higher self.

I might have shocked you at the beginning of this chapter with my frankness. However, the story I used to recite to myself no longer has any energy. It is boring. If I were to say those words now as though they were still the story I was living, I would squirm inside, telling me that I am just saying it for the sake of it. In fact, I knew I had re-written my story one day many, many years ago when I did tell my old story and I did squirm. That was the last time I did so. I knew then that I was operating because of habit without my soul awareness. Now, putting those experiences to better use, they are part of the past, unless used as a teaching tool, and even then, it feels as though it was a very different me who had those experiences. You may experience this too in your own way.

Through the insights I am sharing in this book, the techniques and the exercises, I have learned and explored my journey to the point where my past is a feature of my empowerment, creativity and joy. Without my past experiences my understanding of others' situations and circumstances would leave me feeling like a fraud. With them I am limitless.

Have you started to re-write your story? There is only now, so live it to the fullest from your heart.

Affirmations . . . .

- I have easily released all past hurt
- I infuse myself with love from Source
- I am free
- I honour myself in everything I do, say and believe
- Deep at the centre of myself there is an infinite source of love that is always readily available to me.

*The Soul
Whisperer's guide
to becoming
Light-filled,
Loving and Wise*

How to be your own Soul Whisperer . . . .

If you could choose just one day from your past and harvest its positive emotions and memories as though they were golden nectar of the highest potency, what day would you choose? Maybe you would have a variety to choose from. You will recognise which ones really are meaningful for you by the heart-sing feelings it stirs in you. You may have experience of your higher self in this situation. Perhaps you feel you have yet to experience it. If this is your case, imagine what would create a day such as this and feel it make your heart sing.

Becoming your own Soul Whisperer is unmistakably part of the journey for this lifetime. This adventure into infusing your self-knowing and intuition through the Weaver of Wisdom, known as your higher self, brings rewards that cover a broad spectrum. This scale ranges from releasing negative emotions and limiting beliefs to generating greater confidence, self-esteem, inner peace, unconditional love and freely trusting your infinite source of wisdom.

As you have engaged in the exercises, tips, hints and affirmations within the preceding chapters, you have, layer by layer, been removing the fears and illusions that have been shrouding your life thus far. In its place you have awakened a deeper sense of love and self-honouring, connection with your intuition, a willingness to meet change and embrace many opportunities to grow.

Most of all, you will have started to unite more firmly with the attributes of your soul that will always guide you in your best interest through the rest of your life. This is now part of your 'weave'.

You may need to revisit some of the chapters and this is what I would expect. Remember that you are clearing years, if not lifetimes, of baggage. Go gently on yourself. There is a real opportunity to create a better life. If your emotions start to get the better of you, then let them have their turn and clear what they hold. Your soul will always return you to balance.

By allowing your intuitive senses to come alive, you are infusing yourself with quality information that is intended just for you and is designed to heal, enrich and inspire you. By letting your imagination out to play, you are opening the doorway to the source of creativity that brought you here in the first place. By listening to your inner voice you will always have the best consultant working with you 24/7.

When your heart sings you will hear your soul sigh with relief, as feelings of joy and bliss radiate through you and out to the world. When you live as your higher self you send out a huge ripple that positively embraces and influences all around you.

What makes all of this possible is the choice you made to become your own Soul Whisperer.

This is an exciting path of learning to understand yourself and your soul's journey. In doing so, your life purpose and its path have greater clarity, meaning and are infused with continual inspiration, happiness, love, health and peace.

Becoming Light-filled, Loving and Wise

The Soul Whisperer's guide to empowered living . . .

- Employ your soulistic consciousness in every situation
- Recognise fear as an illusion
- Let go of expectation, self-sabotage and criticism
- Let others be responsible for themselves, their choices and their experiences
- Detach from the need to control the outcome of a situation
- Look, listen and speak in the same proportion as your eyes, ears and mouth
- Beliefs are what you choose and must serve your highest good (Weaver of Wisdom) otherwise they are limitations
- Release all limitation by recognising the lesson
- Know that your free will makes all the difference
- Know that you are enough
- What you see outside yourself is a reflection of what you hold within you, make your world beautiful as you are on the inside
- Know yourself to be your own Soul Whisperer and use all the attributes contained within this book to release yourself from fear and illusion
- Love yourself because of your differences, rather than in spite of them
- Love others for the same reason.

The Soul Code – the secrets to being your own Soul Whisperer . . . .

- Your soul tangibly communicates through your inner sense of your heart sing (and your gut clench)
- Everything and every thought makes an impact on you/ your soul
- Even the small daily interactions that give rise to a feeling within you have an impact
- Every time you feel frustration, anger, annoyance, fear or any other heavy emotion, your heart/soul shuts down temporarily
- Connecting with your heart-sing sense allows you to recognise what is in your highest good
- Acting on what makes your heart sing keeps you in close communication with your soul purpose
- When you follow your soul purpose your life gains clarity.
- Having clarity gives you greater confidence, self-esteem, self-respect, direction, meaning, empowerment and inspiration
- You make choices that enrich and enhance your daily life thus making your world a source of continual joy, happiness and abundance.

Ultimately, following the Soul Code, means that you experience greater love, inner peace, creativity and life satisfaction, free from illusion and fear.

You are at a point of complete opportunity. Consider how wonderful, inspired, empowered, enriched and enchanted your life will be when you unlock your Soul Code and become your own Soul Whisperer. Start today. Start now.

Power affirmations for empowerment and release . . . .

Choose the most appropriate affirmation(s) that reflect your present need for growth and repeat regularly, with feeling and belief, until you notice the changes around you. When you start forgetting to say your affirmation, chances are you no longer need it.

Be conscious of the changes happening around and within you, this will show you the next direction or action to take. I totally support your continued growth, empowerment, happiness and enriched journey, now and always. Namaste.

Abandonment – I am safe, supported and surrounded with love.

Abuse – I am in control. I am honoured by those around me.

Anger – I express my emotions positively.

Anxiety – I am calm. I am in control of my circumstances.

Attachments disorders – Who I am is enough. I am whole and complete.

Choice – I am master of my choices. I confidently make the best possible choices with the guidance of my soul.

Confidence – Everyday I congratulate myself for being me. I love myself. I journey through life with confidence and ease. I trust myself.

Criticism – I love myself as I am. Who I am is enough.

Depression – I release all withheld anger with grace and ease.

Disappointment – Life happens as it is meant to, all is well.

Emotional blackmail – I am the master of my emotions and experiences.

Emotional pain – I release the need to carry emotional pain, I choose to be healed, whole and complete.

Failure – I am open to opportunity.

Fear – I release all false evidence that appears real.

Fear of success – I trust myself and my abilities.

Guilt – Only I can make me feel a certain way.

Happiness – I embrace every opportunity for happiness.

Humiliation – My experiences make me stronger.

Heartbreak – I fulfil all my needs easily. I release all emotional pain.

Hopelessness – I matter. I love myself. Who I am makes a positive difference.

Intuition – I easily experience the messages from my soul. I act on my soul messages with trust.

Isolation – I am supported by the Universe. I am always in good company.

Jealously – I am responsible for my own life, success, happiness and love.

Knowing yourself – I accept myself just as I am.

Learning to laugh – My laughter lights up my heart and my world. It is safe to be happy.

Loss – Loss is an illusion. Loved ones are always alive in my heart.

Love – I am love. I know how to love. I know how to receive love.

Love of self – I love myself just as I am.

Lovable – I deserve to be loved. I attract only genuine love.

Love starvation – I love myself therefore I am always loved.

Manipulated – I know how to remain in my own integrity.

Manipulation – I release the need to manipulate. I express my needs with confidence.

Mistrust – I trust my intuition. I trust myself.

Negativity – I turn all possibilities into opportunities.

Neglect – I am strong. I am whole and complete.

Over-sensitivity – I am safe.

Parenting your parents – Parents are people too. I love them for who they are.

Reassurance – I am always cared for, supported and guided in life. I trust my intuition.

Rejection – I love and accept myself for who I am.

Relationships – I create loving, supportive and healthy relationships.

Resentment – I release all expectation. I am responsible for my own feelings.

Self-respect – I respect myself for who I am. I forgive myself for previous acts.

Self-sabotage – I am worthy of living a joy filled, loving, successful, empowering life.

Self-sacrifice – I matter.

Self-worth – I am worthy of respect, love, happiness and joy every day.

Shame – I forgive myself for my actions and learn from them.

Soul betrayal – I release those who have betrayed me and send them love.

Soul whispering – I am my own Soul Whisperer. I clearly receive the wisdom for my highest good from within.

Suffering – I stop all suffering within myself now and replace it with support.

Trust – I trust myself. I remain in tune with my intuition always.

Victim – I release the need to be a victim. I honour myself as I am.

Vulnerable – I am safe. I am supported. I know who I am.

And finally, there is one affirmation that you might consider saying everyday as you wake and get ready for sleep – I am light-filled, loving and wise – I am.

About the Author . . . .

Anna-Louise Haigh's career within the therapy, healing and empowerment arena has earned her unique distinction. Her distinguishing hallmarks include delivering personal growth opportunities with compassion, sensitivity and passion. Her natural ease and approachability coupled with her reputation for empowering, inspiring and facilitating change have infused her global audiences with the tools for transformation.

Building on a hugely successful career in complementary therapies that includes developing a new modality, Daoyin Tao – Chinese face, neck and shoulder massage, Anna-Louise is a certified Soul and Past-Life Coach, Soul Midwife (in service to incoming and outgoing souls as they birth into the life that awaits them), Theta DNA Practitioner and Advanced Training Facilitator. Anna-Louise is the creator of the transformative Soulistic Makeover experience and Soul Love Awakening journeywork for a better life on all levels.

Her workshops, retreats, courses and international speaking opportunities are a natural extension of the results she witnesses within her private consultations. The demand for her work parallels the ever increasing need for individuals to find answers, meaning and direction. Anna-Louise delivers from the heart.

As an international speaker in high demand she has many requests to travel the globe to deliver inspiring and life-changing opportunities. Owing to demand, she offers telephone consultations to ensure that distances are dissolved. Along with this, she sees private clients at her consulting rooms in Harrogate, North Yorkshire, England. Through her websites and blog it is possible to receive continual inspiration, learn about workshops, courses, retreats and e-programmes all aimed at enriching your life.

Opportunities with Anna-Louise . . . . . .

Free Affirmation creation service – simply email your request for a powerful affirmation to help you move forward to affirmations@anna-louise.com.

Soul Empowerment Consultations and the Soulistic Makeover experience are available globally by phone or in person by contacting Anna-Louise through her websites
www.anna-louise.com or
www.anna-louisehaigh.com.

Also available: Inspired SOULutions talks, company presentations, workshops, events, retreats, lectures and keynote speaking globally.

Regular Soul Empowerment and Inspired SOULutions tele-seminars and e-learning programmes.

For further information please email:
empowerment@anna-louise.com

Full details of events and opportunities for personal growth are available at:
www.anna-louise.com
www.anna-louisehaigh.com
www.SecretsOfUnlimitedLiving.com
www.learntheta.com
Blog: http://inspiredsoulutions.wordpress.com
Be a fan on Facebook: Anna-Louise The Soul Whisperer

Resources . . . .
Terry Loveland (Bowen) – www.terrybowen.com
Denise Linn – www.soulcoaching.com